Words of Praise for *Burn Brightly Without Burning Out*

Does balance exist between your professional and private life? For most of us it is a struggle. In *Burn Brightly Without Burning Out,* Richard Biggs shares with us his insight and presents encouraging ways to make the transition to a more balanced life, one that is focused on being, rather than thinking and doing.

—KEN BLANCHARD, COAUTHOR OF
THE ONE MINUTE MANAGER® AND *WHALE DONE!*™

Burn Brightly Without Burning Out will help you realize that the important things in life are free, and stimulate your motivation to cultivate their presence in your life—and, as a by-product, become a super-successful human being!

—RUTH STAFFORD PEALE,
CHAIRMAN, *GUIDEPOSTS*

What do you need to change in your life? Are you burning brightly or burning out in the spiritual, mental, physical, or emotional sides of your life? Do you long for better balance between the work you need and the life you lead?

If your answers reveal a need for improvement, I urge you to read this book from cover to cover. Take notes. Develop action plans. Most important, make a vow to implement any changes—starting right now! It just might be the best decision you've ever made.

—JOHN C. MAXWELL,
LEADERSHIP EXPERT AND AUTHOR OF
THE 21 IRREFUTABLE LAWS OF LEADERSHIP

BURN BRIGHTLY

WITHOUT BURNING OUT

BURN BRIGHTLY
WITHOUT BURNING OUT

*Balancing the Work You Need
with the Life You Lead*

RICHARD K. BIGGS

THOMAS NELSON PUBLISHERS®
Nashville

A Division of Thomas Nelson, Inc.
www.ThomasNelson.com

Published in Nashville, Tennessee, by Thomas Nelson, Inc.

The Scripture quotations are from the *Holy Bible,* New Living Translation, copyright © 1996. Used by permission of Tyndale House Publishers, Inc., Wheaton, Illinois 60189. All rights reserved.

Graphics by Catherine Manning of Printworks of Atlanta.

Library of Congress Cataloging-in-Publication Data

Biggs, Richard K.
 Burn brightly without burning out : balancing the work you need with the life you lead / Richard K. Biggs.
  p. cm.
 ISBN 0-7852-6513-9 (hardcover)
 1. Job satisfaction. 2. Burn out (Psychology) 3. Conduct of life I. Title.
HF5549.5.J63 B4844 2002
158.7—dc21   2002008754

Printed in the United States of America

1 2 3 4 5 6 BVG 05 04 03 02

This book is dedicated to the many mentors who have come into my life and provided guidance, wisdom, encouragement, and prayers. Some of them are mentioned in the pages that follow; others remain unnamed, but they know who they are. Thank you for investing in my life and believing in me. As these life lessons are passed on to others, I hope the impact will be even greater than the difference you've made in my life. God bless you always.

CONTENTS

FOREWORD

I had the privilege of meeting Dick Biggs not long after we moved The INJOY Group from San Diego to Atlanta. We connected right away. Dick is a trusted friend, eager protégé, fellow speaker, and Christian brother.

I listen to Dick because he's an idea man. I appreciate his thinking, life experiences, and deep desire to help others be the best they can be. I love the big message of this little book. Whether you're struggling to find work/life balance, or seeking to better the quality of life you now enjoy, Dick can help you.

Howard Hendricks, a good friend and legendary teacher at Dallas Theological Seminary, says: "Balance is going from one extreme to the other." Dick has been on both extremes of life's difficult balancing act. He burned out from living a radically unbalanced life. And he nearly burned out from trying to live a perfectly balanced life.

As a result of his struggles, Dick has learned some valuable lessons. Through his masterful storytelling style, Dick examines twenty of life's most delicate contrasts and makes them relevant. Each chapter reveals a timeless truth, offers practical application tips, and issues a call to action. This is must reading for anyone seeking a more balanced lifestyle.

During lunch before our company Christmas party in 1998, Dick and I discussed physical discipline—a weak area for me at that time. Dick, an avid runner who has completed seven marathons, talked briefly about the importance of regular exercise and proper diet. I wish we'd had this talk a lot earlier, because I suffered a heart attack a few days later. I nearly burned out permanently. This defining moment led to a change in my eating habits and the start of a daily exercise routine.

What do you need to change in your life? Are you burning brightly or burning out in the spiritual, mental, physical, or emotional sides of your life? Do you long for better balance between the work you need and the life you lead?

If your answers reveal a need for improvement, I urge you to read this book from cover to cover. Take notes. Develop action plans. Most important, make a vow to implement any changes—starting right now! It just might be the best decision you've ever made.

Two years after my heart attack, Dick and I were swapping Christmas presents. He gave me a very special gift—a beautiful plaque in tribute to our mentoring relationship. I cherish this thoughtful memento, but I value our friendship even more. I've learned a lot from my protégé. You can learn from Dick, too, if you'll apply the priceless wisdom of *Burn Brightly Without Burning Out.*

Dr. John C. Maxwell
Founder, The INJOY Group
Atlanta, Georgia

INTRODUCTION

A cheerful heart is good medicine, but a broken spirit saps a person's strength.

—PROVERBS 17:22

Are you burning brightly with a cheerful heart? Or are you burning out with a broken spirit?

The American workforce of the twenty-first century has more money and affluence than any generation in history. Workaholics abound. They've bought into the idea that no successful business-person can achieve balance in life. The so-called rat race is in high gear, but the pace of the competition has left many workers exhausted and disillusioned.

In short, people are stressed out and burned out. They're yearning for more personal and family time. They're questioning whether work/life balance is fact or fantasy. They're out of control. Yet some people are discovering that faith and spirituality can be the source of well-being and balance in their lives. Here's a sampling of the evidence:

- AON Consulting conducted a workforce survey of 1,800 people to determine employee loyalty in America. This study identified seventeen key factors or "drivers" of workforce loyalty. The No. 1 driver was "management's recognition of the importance of personal and family time."[1]

- A *Fast Company* story titled "No Work, No Life, No Kidding" stated that people are "wondering if there really is any way to 'balance' work and family."[2]

- A *Fortune* cover read: "God and Business . . . The Surprising Quest for Spiritual Renewal in the American Workplace."[3]

- *The Kiplinger Letter,* commenting on corporate scandals such as Enron, WorldCom, and others, said: "More job seekers will consider company culture, not just the pay."[4]

- Kathleen Parker, a syndicated columnist for *Tribune Media Services,* wrote in an editorial shortly after the September 11, 2001, terrorist attacks on the World Trade Center Towers in New York City and the Pentagon in Washington, D.C.: "One can't help notice the silence of atheists these days. America today is about God and country, but then it always has been. We just lost track."[5]

The message is loud and clear. Demanding careers are interfering with time for personal interests, others, and concern for spiritual fulfillment. Biblical wisdom, which has stood the test of time for 3,500 years, says there are severe consequences for people who think life is only about work and professional success. King Solomon learned this lesson the hard way.

Known as the wisest man who ever lived, Solomon spent most of his years acquiring success, material possessions, authority, fame, and pleasure. Near the end of his life, Solomon lamented, "As I looked at everything I had worked so hard to accomplish, it was all so meaningless. It was like chasing the wind. There was nothing really worthwhile anywhere" (Eccl. 2:11).

Can you identify with Solomon? I can. My parents were Salvation Army officers who taught me the importance of serving others and God. When I left home to join the Marines, I strayed from the biblical values of my childhood and spent many of my adult years chasing the wind of secularism. Like Solomon, I was left with a broken spirit. I was thirty-seven before returning to my roots.

After the Marines I spent a year as a starving sportswriter before choosing a more lucrative career. For thirteen years I was a high-earning salesman and sales manager. I burned out so badly, I quit my job and didn't work for five months.

On the outside I appeared happy. After all, I possessed many so-called tangibles of success. On the inside, though, I was miserable. I was living an incredibly unbalanced life focused on me, money, materialism, and mega-hours at work.

In 1982 I experienced the most radical turning point of my life. Within a ten-week span, I started a business and met the woman who would become my wife two years later. Entrepreneurship helped me realize there's more to career satisfaction than making money. Judy helped me return to my spiritual foundation.

From the ashes of personal burnout and failure came a life that began to burn brightly.

For eighteen frustrating years, I was driven by the *haves* of a materialistic world. This quest influenced my *thinking* and *doing*. I failed to *be* true to myself, to others, and to God. It was an unbalanced lifestyle based on have ⟶ think ⟶ do ⟶ be.

That burnout is gone forever. For the past twenty-one years, I've endeavored to live a more balanced life by *being* faithful to spiritual truths. This way of life has influenced my *thinking* and *doing*. My *haves* extend beyond material things to intangible blessings. It's a balanced lifestyle based on be ⟶ think ⟶ do ⟶ have.

Yes, it's okay to have nice possessions, money in the bank, professional success, and fun times. I enjoy all of these things. It's just that when these tangibles were the center of my life, I had a broken spirit. I was a burned-out man.

Today, I'm driven by a deep faith in God. I'm motivated to serve others.

I'm determined to maintain my integrity. I have a cheerful heart, for I'm burning brightly.

Does this mean there won't be struggles after adopting a more balanced lifestyle? Of course not. I continue to experience my share of difficult challenges, and so will you. We walk a fine line between failure and success, sadness and happiness, unbalanced and balanced living.

Optimum balance requires a careful, consistent monitoring of the delicate contrasts of life. On one end, burnout is virtually assured if you live an unbalanced life. On the other end, expect to be stressed out if you try to live a perfectly balanced life.

The big message of this little book is that you can burn brightly by balancing the work you need with the life you lead. How? You must be intentional about your life.

You can begin by answering life's five greatest questions:

1. *Who* am I?
2. *Why* am I here?
3. *Where* am I going?
4. *How* will I get there?
5. *When* I get there, *what* will I have?

High achievers do a great job answering the third and fourth questions, which relate to preparation and performance. These people are sure they know what they want, and they go after it. Questions one, two, and five are more complex, for they deal with principles, purpose, and perspective. People who answer these questions place a higher priority on being true to themselves and their Creator than trying to impress others. When you can answer all five questions honestly and promptly, you're serious about a better quality of life.

The world is full of successful businesspeople longing for deeper personal fulfillment. Sounds contradictory, doesn't it? Surely professional success and personal happiness go hand in hand, right? Actually they do not. Without a measure of balance, the scales of life become top heavy, and burnout is often the end result. Burned-out people lack balance, which is essential for long-term professional success and personal happiness.

Business achievement tends to be measured by tangibles such as money, possessions, and status. It becomes a futile race to see how much is enough. Personal happiness is more meaningful when measured by intangibles such as inner peace, service to others, and faithfulness to God. It's a difficult balancing act, but the enduring truths of the Bible teach us that cheerful hearts and spirits aren't mutually exclusive.

King Solomon finally realized what matters most in life, and he went from burnout to burning brightly: "Here is my final conclusion: Fear God and obey his commands, for this is the duty of every person. God will judge us for everything we do, including every secret thing, whether good or bad" (Eccl. 12:13–14). His broken spirit was turned into a cheerful heart when Solomon was wise enough to be true to himself, honest with others, and loyal to God.

If your heart is cheerful, this book offers insights to help you keep on burning brightly. If your spirit is broken, you'll discover practical ideas to aid your transition from burnout to burning brightly. No matter how you're feeling, there are how-tos and hope to be found in the following twenty contrasts.

My deepest desire is that you'll read on, learn from these lessons, make any necessary changes, and become the person God has always wanted you to be.

—RICHARD K. BIGGS

1

IMAGE VS. INTEGRITY

Image is what others think you are. Do people have the wrong image of you? Or do they see who you really are?

Integrity is the real you. It means being true to yourself, which is necessary to be honest with others. I witnessed this truth in action several years ago in Texas.

A client hired me to do a host of seminars for the company's sales organizations in cities across America. My topic dealt primarily with ethics and professionalism in sales. On this particular day, I was in Dallas, and the room was filled to capacity.

A young man said to me prior to the session, "Mr. Biggs, I flew in from a little town in Arkansas because I've heard good things about your seminar. I just got promoted from salesman to sales manager, and I can't wait to hear what you have to say about this important topic." My initial image of this young fellow was that he was serious about learning.

The young sales manager sat on the front row, took copious notes, nodded in agreement, and asked thoughtful questions. At the end of the seminar, he shook my hand and thanked me for a wonderful day. Now, my image of this new sales manager had shifted from eager learner to someone who was going to share this message with his sales force.

I packed my seminar bag and walked out into the hotel lobby to catch a cab to the airport. The young man from Arkansas spotted me and inquired, "Mr. Biggs, are you flying out of DFW?" I told him yes, and he asked, "Well, if you don't have other plans, can we ride together, split the cab fare, and talk some more about today's session?" I agreed.

He talked incessantly about the value of ethics and professionalism in sales. He repeated some of the things I'd said. He stressed how valuable the day had been. As we arrived at his terminal, my image of this young man had gone from an eager learner willing to share an important message with his salespeople to, "Wow! I've really had a big influence on this fellow's life."

The fare was forty dollars. We each paid twenty dollars, but the young man asked the cab driver for a forty-dollar receipt. Pocketing the inflated receipt, the sales manager winked at me and boasted, "I learned that trick from my general manager!" I was speechless, but here's what I was thinking en route to my terminal:

- What other "tricks" had his general manager taught him?

- Would he be teaching these "tricks" to his sales force?

- Had he *heard* anything I'd said that day?

My image of this person changed drastically when he failed to be true to himself. He was a man saying one thing and doing another. I was disappointed that my message had so little impact.

Eight years later, and after I had told that story a few hundred times, a woman approached me following a presentation. "Mr. Biggs," she said, "I know who that young man is, and I want to tell you the rest of the story." She identified the man's name, hometown, industry, employer, and what happened to him a few months after the seminar. "The owner found out about the cab fare scam," she explained, "and fired him on the spot. That sales manager got to bragging to his coworkers, and he lost his job over twenty dollars. Isn't that incredible?"

What's really incredible is this leader's loss of *integrity*, a word derived from the Latin *integer*, meaning "undiminished, complete, whole." Integrity is about having sound moral character. It's having your heart in the right place. It means you won't compromise your principles for any reason, including the overpayment of travel reimbursement from your employer.

You know what else is extraordinary about this story? People say, "Dick, he cheated his company out of only twenty dollars. It's no big deal." One guy even asked, "Dick, is that really a true story?" Good grief, how could I make up a story about integrity?

You can't spell *integrity* without the word *grit*:

Grit: "a firmness of mind, unyielding courage" that leads to . . .

Respect: "a high or special regard" by others that fosters . . .

Influence: "which produces an effect without force" based on . . .

Truth: "that which agrees with final reality."

It takes a great deal of grit or courage to be true to yourself, but the rewards are worth it. You gain the immeasurable respect of others, an opportunity to influence them in a positive way, and the satisfaction of knowing your life is based on rock-solid principles. Here are three of my favorite quotes on integrity:

When regard for the truth has broken down or even slightly weakened, all things remain doubtful. (Saint Augustine)

Choose a good reputation over great riches, for being held in high esteem is better than having silver or gold. (Prov. 22:1)

Every man's work . . . is always a portrait of himself, and the more he tries to conceal himself, the more clearly will his character appear in spite of him. (Samuel Butler, *The Way of All Flesh*)

I was apprehensive after leaving journalism to enter the sales profession in 1970. I was uncomfortable with my image of salespeople as fast-talking, high-pressuring, and misleading. A good friend told me to be true to myself and honest with others, and everything else, including my image, would take care of itself. It was wise advice.

You have no control over the unethical or unprofessional behavior of your competitors, but you are in charge of your behavior. Will you maintain your integrity in spite of external influences? Or will you make ethical compromises because "everybody else is doing it"?

Behavior has a price tag. If you choose to be untrue to yourself and dishonest with others, the initial cost will be a worried mind, troubled heart, and restless body. However, the final payment for the shortcuts of life can be a lot higher when caught in the web of self-destruction.

If you choose to be true to yourself and honest with others, the return on your investment is priceless. Honorable people know the joy of inner peace and burning brightly. They understand the awesome responsibility of influencing others as worthy role models and mentors. They value the truths of the Bible and desire to be obedient to God, who created us in His impeccable image.

Integrity is a unique way of life. It can't be taken from you, but you can give it away as the Arkansas sales manager did. Will you be more concerned with your image and, in the process, give away your integrity? Or will you be true to yourself and retain the most precious asset you have?

It's a decision with radical consequences. Choose integrity, and your image will take care of itself.

2

MISSION VS. PURPOSE

A mission is a series of tangible, short-term activities. A military mission is an example of a team effort, but an individual can also be "on a mission." When these team or individual activities are completed, the mission is over, and a new one begins.

A purpose is an intangible, long-term expression of why a person or organization exists. Purpose gives lifetime meaning to what you do, personally or professionally. Missions change continuously. A purpose, when conceived at a mature enough level, remains constant.

I don't know whether the following story is true or a tall tale, but it certainly illustrates the vast difference between mission and purpose. A high school quarterback was playing the last game of his illustrious career. For the team, the state championship was at stake. For the quarterback, there was an opportunity to break the state record for career pass completions by a high-schooler.

The game was a defensive struggle. With ten seconds left to play, the star quarterback's team led 10 to 6 and was on its opponent's 5-yard line. With the other team out of timeouts and the state title at hand, the quarterback stopped the clock and ran to the sideline.

"Young man," said the furious coach, "I know what you're thinking. You've tied the passing record, and you'd like one more chance to break it. This team championship, though, is more important than your personal record. You go out there, drop to one knee, and let the clock expire. Whatever you do, don't pass the football. Do you understand me, son?"

The temptation proved too great for the quarterback, who called a conservative pass play: "You wide receivers take one step out, then two steps back. I'll throw a quick sideline pattern to one of you. Just catch the ball and fall to the ground. We'll be champions, and the pass record will be mine."

The quarterback dropped back and fired a quick strike to his wide receiver in the right flat. Unfortunately the quarterback forgot to freeze the defense by looking left or up the middle. In the excitement of the moment, he never took his eye off his right-side receiver.

The left cornerback read the play, stepped in front of the wide receiver, and intercepted the pass. The state title hung in the balance. The defensive back had 95 yards of open field ahead of him. And he was the state champion in the 100 meters.

The only thing in the quarterback's favor was a good angle of pursuit. He took off after the interceptor—the 50 . . . 40 . . . 30 . . . 20 . . . 10. In desperation the quarterback made a game-saving tackle at the five-yard line. The state championship was secured, and the quarterback had tied the career pass completion record.

The media surrounded the hero as he came off the field. A reporter asked, "Son, how in the world did you catch that defensive back? Don't you know he's the state champion in the 100 meters?"

The quarterback smiled confidently and replied, "Sir, that defensive back was running to score the winning touchdown. I was running to save my life!"

You see, that defensive back was on a mission to score the winning touchdown. It was tangible and short-term, because once the play was over, so was the mission. On the other hand, that quarterback was on-purpose. He was thinking about more than the game-saving play. He was concerned with the intangible, long-term potential of his lifetime.

What about your life? Do you know why you are here? If the answer is yes, you are to be congratulated. If not, why not?

The best way to know your purpose is to create a written statement, and here's *why*. A purpose statement . . .

- demands a sorting out of what's important.
- provides clear direction.
- offers sharp focus.
- builds morale.
- requires long-term thinking.
- contributes meaning and significance to life.
- simplifies decision making.
- affords a valuable tool for evaluation and accountability.

Now, here's *how* to craft your purpose statement:

1. *Find a guiding principle as an anchor.* You might use a line from a poem, an inspirational quote, a Scripture verse, or anything else that sets the tone for your life's purpose.

2. *Make a list of your dominant interests.* These are the major areas of your life where you spend your days (more on this in Chapter 3).

3. *List the qualities you admire most in your role models and mentors.* Some sample qualities include integrity, reliability, patience, wisdom, discipline, and a positive attitude.

4. *State your strongest character qualities.* It's okay if some of the qualities are the same as the ones listed in Step 3.

5. *Jot down key phrases you feel should be a part of this document.* Sample phrases include "making a difference," "leaving a lasting legacy," "living passionately," "daring to dream," "choosing wisely," "being socially responsible," "serving the community," "honoring God," and, well, you get the idea.

6. *Make an outline.* Having an outline will save you time and improve the clarity of your statement. My guiding principle, which you'll find below, provided a three-part outline.

7. *Prepare a rough draft.* It's time to incorporate your thoughts from Steps 1 through 6 into a preliminary purpose statement. Don't be concerned with spelling, grammar, or word length. Just get your thoughts on paper for what could become the most important document of your life.

8. *Edit, rewrite, and polish.* Crystallize your thinking. Chop your words. Carve out a way of life that's uniquely you. Create a masterpiece using as few words as possible.

9. *Ask for feedback from trusted friends or relatives.* What do they like about your statement? How can it be improved? Integrate any changes until you're satisfied with your life's purpose.

10. *Put the finished document in prominent places and refer to it often.* Read it regularly, lest it be filed and forgotten. You might memorize these words over time, but the idea is to live your life so purposefully that the people around you could almost recite your statement.

My purpose statement is anchored by Micah 6:8, a guiding principle that says, "The LORD has already told you what is good, and this is what he requires: to do what is right, to love mercy, and to walk humbly with your God."

Purpose Statement of Dick Biggs

Personal

I will strive "to do what is right" by maintaining integrity in all facets of my daily living.

Others

I will strive "to love mercy" by having a positive influence on others as a principle-centered role model and mentor.

God

I will strive "to walk humbly with . . . God" through congruency between my beliefs and behavior.

What are you waiting for? You have the *whys* and *hows* for creating your purpose and a sample statement. Why not vow to complete your purpose statement in the next thirty days? I promise you it will make a tremendous difference in your life.

Will you do me a favor? Once you've completed your purpose statement (or one for your organization), please send me a copy so I'll know you took action. I've been collecting these documents for years. I have scores of letters attesting to the incredible power of a written purpose. Please forward your statements and comments to

> BOLD!
> 9615 Settlers Lane
> Gainesville, GA 30506
> biggspeaks@mindspring.com

Just like that young quarterback, be more on-purpose. You'll be better balanced. Best of all, you'll burn more brightly than ever.

3

MANAGING TIME VS. MANAGING DOMINANT INTERESTS

The key to a balanced lifestyle is the proper control of where you spend your time. But first let's distinguish between managing time and managing dominant interests. Time management is how you allocate the hours of each day to your dominant interests. For example, Monday might demand nine hours at work. Saturday might include six hours of family time. Sunday might require three hours at your place of worship.

Dominant interests management is how you choose the major areas of your life where you spend your days. Are you a one-dimensional workaholic? Or are you making time to balance your career with the rest of your life?

To help with this difficult challenge, I suggest you develop a dominant interests chart. Here's mine:

Some major activities within each dominant interest include:

God

- Doing daily devotionals
- Studying the Bible
- Attending church
- Participating in small-group activities
- Tithing
- Sharing my faith

Others

- Spending time with my wife, stepdaughters, grandson, and other family members
- Developing friendships
- Mentoring in my community and elsewhere

Personal

- Operating my business
- Exercising, relaxing, reading, vacationing, etc.
- Handling financial matters

We all have diverse dominant interests, so create a unique chart to clarify your lifestyle focus. The ideal number of dominant interests is between three and seven. With less than three, you'll probably be out of balance. With more than seven, you're likely to be stressed out, even burned out.

Don't worry if a particular day is out of balance due to a heavy workload or family emergency. Strive for weekly, monthly, quarterly, or even yearly balance. If you haven't spent time in each area periodically, reassess your dominant interests, or strive for better time management.

Of course there's no such thing as perfect balance. In fact, if you try to live a perfectly balanced life every single day, you will fail. There will be days when balance means . . .

- working longer hours.

- spending time with family and friends.

- exercising or relaxing.

- doing a community project.

- growing spiritually.

For years, my weakest dominant interest was in the area of community. I couldn't find an organization that agreed with my schedule. I felt guilty. How could community be a dominant interest if I wasn't spending time in this area?

I kept hearing about my local school mentor program. The commitment was only one hour a week with a student. A brochure explained the rewards of the program and mentioned a shortage of mentors, especially men. I attended a training class to get a closer look.

Dr. Kennedy Smartt, who mentors five boys, was a guest speaker at this session. He talked about the privilege of mentoring kids and making a difference in their lives. I had lunch with Kennedy and got involved.

The counselor at McEver Elementary told me about Scotty Cole, a seven-year-old repeating the first grade. "Scotty is a real sweet boy," she said, "but he needs to work on his self-confidence. I think you'll be just what he needs."

I'll always cherish the day we met. Scotty wore glasses, had thick blond hair, and seemed anxious for a mentor. We connected immediately. We spent our time talking, reading, playing ball, having fun on the computer, and repeating the following exchange every week:

DICK: What are goals?

SCOTTY: Goals are things you want to do and places you want to go.

DICK: That's right. And what is confidence?

SCOTTY: Confidence means you can do something.

DICK: And what will negative people tell you?

SCOTTY: They'll say I can't do it.

DICK: So what do you say to these people?

SCOTTY: I tell them I can do it . . . unless it's something stupid or bad.

One day while we were in the library, a bearded man approached us. He identified himself as a photographer with the *Gainesville Times* and wanted to know what we were doing. I told him about our protégé-mentor relationship. The photographer took our picture.

Scotty and I made the newspaper later that week. I delivered several copies to the school. Scotty was so excited. When I returned the following week, the clipping was posted on the school bulletin board. At the end of the year, I wrote a column about our experience, and it was published in the *Times*.

Scotty's confidence grew steadily. His teacher, counselor, and principal asked often, "What are you doing to make such a difference in Scotty?" My simple answer was, "I'm spending time with him."

Scotty moved to Myers Elementary in the second grade. This trip required forty more minutes of driving for me, but I continued to mentor Scotty because my small investment of time was producing big results. At the end of our second year together, Scotty gave me a plaque that reads:

> *One hundred years from now,*
> *It will not matter*
> *What kind of car I drove,*
> *What kind of house I lived in,*
> *How much money I had in my bank account,*
> *Nor what my clothes looked like.*
> *But the world may be a little better*
> *Because I was important in the life of a child.*

We're now in our fourth year together. Scotty has memorized my phone number and calls often. He invites me to his birthday parties and church activities. I send him postcards from across America. I buy him gifts for special occasions.

When the demands of my other dominant interests tend to clash, I remember what Scotty says about having a mentor:

- "You're always there on Mondays. If you have to travel, you let me know."

- "You really care about me."

- "You ask me about my goals for school and at home."

- "You talk with my teacher, especially when I mess up."

- "You write about me in the newspaper."

- "You buy me cool gifts."

- "You let me use the computer and play in the gym."

- "You give me money for ice cream."

Selecting dominant interests means nothing if you're not spending time in these areas. You must be accountable to burn brightly. At the end of life, there should be no regrets about where you spent your short time on earth.

Has one dominant interest taken control of your life? Are you working too much and spending too little time with your family and friends? Do you long for a Scotty Cole experience in your community? Does your spiritual life need a boost? Do you need to get in shape physically or fiscally? Alas, do you yearn for a more balanced lifestyle?

It's all about the meticulous monitoring of your dominant interests and the hours you devote to each one. If you don't take charge of your life, others will. First, pay attention to *where* you spend your days. Second, decide *how* you'll allocate the hours of each day to your dominant interests. It's the key to burning brightly.

4

ROLE MODELING VS. MENTORING

A *role model* is "a person whose behavior in a particular role is imitated by others." A *mentor* is "a trusted counselor, guide, tutor, or coach."

Role modeling isn't optional since you don't choose to be admired; you're chosen. The only question is: Are you setting a positive or negative example? Mentoring is optional because you can say yes or no to a protégé. The only question is: If you don't get involved, who will?

When you're a role model, the primary focus is on you, and the time commitment is simply the life you lead. When you're a mentor, the primary focus is on the protégé, and the time commitment is a deeper personal involvement.

A role model says, "Here's a way to live that you might want to emulate." A mentor says, "Here's a way to live that you might want to emulate . . . and let me share the details of my journey."

Mentoring is a way to take role modeling to the next level by teaching protégés the specifics of who you *are,* how you *think,* what you've *done,* and why you *have* something worth pursuing. Life has interesting ways of turning role models into mentors.

In 1998 I spoke at a major dental conference in Atlanta. At the end of my program, I was greeted by Dr. Gerald Maize of Franklin, North

Carolina: "Dick, your teaching style and philosophy of life remind me of John Maxwell. I'm going to send you one of his books. Are you familiar with John?"

I'd heard John speak at a Promise Keepers' meeting a couple of years before and knew he was the founder of INJOY. I told Dr. Maize how impressed I'd been with John's message. At that point in time, John was a distant role model. About a week later, I received a copy of *The Success Journey.* On page one, John said, "This book is dedicated to the employees of INJOY who are going with me [from San Diego] to Atlanta." Here was a golden opportunity to get to know John on a more personal level.

I'm a connoisseur of master mentors—people who've hammered out their lives on the anvil of goodness, wisdom, experience, and maturity, and are willing to share these lessons with proactive protégés. John couldn't say yes if I didn't ask.

I called Atlanta information and was given the telephone number for INJOY. Linda Eggers, John's able personal assistant, arranged a lunch appointment. John and I met three months later, and our relationship has blossomed.

We have a standing lunch appointment every six months. We worship at North Point Community Church in Alpharetta, Georgia. I've shared ideas that John has used in his books and tape clubs. John refers me speaking engagements he can't get to due to his busy schedule. We're working on other mutual projects.

When John's office refers speaking leads my way, I'm impressed by this man's powerful influence. INJOY sends out a cover letter explaining why John can't accept a speaking engagement and recommending me as a replacement. Meeting planners often say, "If John thinks that highly of you, Dick, that's good enough for me."

One of the remarkable things about John is that he takes notes when we get together. Here's a man who has several honorary doctorates and was a pastor for twenty-five years. He has written more than twenty books, including *The 21 Irrefutable Laws of Leadership*, a *New York Times* best-seller. He has produced scores of audio and video training programs. He speaks all over the world to millions of people. He employs more than one hundred people, and most of his key people followed him from California to Georgia.

John not only teaches his protégés, but he also learns from them. It's a privilege to spend time with him. He's a master mentor. By this I refer to people who possess these four lifetime benchmarks:

Benchmark 1: Master mentors pursue what is true.

Who better to help you discover the truths of life than mentors who've already lived them? Mentoring is a way for protégés to shorten their learning curves and accelerate their growth by developing close relationships with seasoned guides on the job, in the community, at your place of worship, or within your family.

Master mentors know that principles determine your beliefs, beliefs determine who you are, and who you are should be based on the truth. Protégés are taught to be principle-centered people by believing in proven, permanent laws for human conduct that have stood the test of time.

Benchmark 2: Master mentors turn creeds into deeds.

Since it's more difficult to model exemplary behavior than recite beliefs, a mentor shows the way and helps you deal more effectively with the daily struggle "to walk your talk." Protégés learn how to go beyond professing to performing by observing people who've already experienced success that really matters.

Creeds without deeds are merely good intentions. Deeds without creeds are recipes for disaster. It takes noble creeds and worthwhile deeds to truly have a cheerful heart.

Benchmark 3: Master mentors use congruence to influence.

Without congruency between creeds and deeds, there is hypocrisy and no credibility. A mentor is a pillar of positive influence, providing protégés with a model of consistency between words and ways.

Protégés learn how to influence people through a caring heart, gentle spirit, and inspiring mind. Mentors understand why coercive persuasion is selfish, manipulative, and counterproductive.

Benchmark 4: Master mentors collect a deep respect.

Mentors earn respect through a lifetime of practicing what they preach. Dr. Michael Guido says that if you remove the *p* from preach, you have reach. If you delete the *r* from reach, you have each. Mentors reach each protégé through teaching at a personal level that fosters admiration and emulation.

President Abraham Lincoln, perhaps the most highly regarded American president, showed his admiration for respect when he said, "If you once forfeit the confidence of your fellow citizens, you can never regain their respect and esteem."

I have five master mentors and four protégés who provide distinct teaching and learning opportunities. As a proactive protégé, you accept the baton of lifelong learning from your mentors. As a master mentor, you pass on the baton of your lifetime lessons to proactive protégés. It's a win-win situation for everyone.

Jesus is my choice as the all-time master mentor. He demonstrated these four benchmarks better than anyone I've ever observed. Whom do you like as your all-time master mentor? Who are your current mentors? Who are your future mentors? Who are you mentoring? Are you striving to pass on wisdom to your protégés?

One of the best ways to burn brightly is to surround yourself with people who are on fire with the enthusiasm of living, loving, and learning. John Maxwell is that kind of mentor. I urge you to take your personal growth and professional development to new heights with the one-on-one leadership concept of mentoring.

5

GENERAL INFORMATION VS. SPECIALIZED KNOWLEDGE

General information is the focus of your early school years. You're taught history, geography, mathematics, writing, and other basics. It's the shotgun approach to learning, which is necessary to be well-rounded academically.

Later, the focus shifts to specialized knowledge. The goal is to learn all you can about a specific field of study. It's the rifle approach to learning, which is essential to acquire a particular expertise.

When I went from sportswriter to salesman, I had a lot of general information but no specialized knowledge of the sales profession. As a journalist I relied on my limited writing skills and love of sports. It was fun working for the Associated Press, but I was eking out a living on $400 a month.

In January 1970, my first month in sales, I made $1,600 with no specialized training. I earned more than $20,000 that year. This "overnight success" had nothing to do with my sales skills and everything to do with my sales manager, who shepherded my every move. I was blinded by this sudden prosperity; my head swelled, and I failed to give the boss his rightful credit.

Have you ever seen an arrogant salesperson? I was so cocky, I could strut sitting down. Then I had the good fortune of doing business with Jim Porterfield. Two days after the sale, Jim called and said, "Dick, you have a lot of talent, and I'm delighted to be one of your customers. But I've been wondering how much better you could be with some formal sales training. I'd like to talk with you about developing your full sales potential."

His comments made me furious. The nerve of this guy telling me I needed sales training after such a tremendous first year. Who does he think he is? Well, Jim worked for Sales Training, Inc., or STI. "We have a five-month training course designed to take you to the next level in sales," explained Jim. "Your investment is $1,100, Dick, and our next class starts in a week. Why not take advantage of this opportunity to learn and grow?"

I fought Jim all the way. His course wasn't necessary because I knew what I was doing. I was already earning an excellent income. I was working too many hours and didn't have time for training. I'd rather invest the money elsewhere.

The consummate professional, Jim Porterfield had done his homework and handled my objections: "You'll be even better after taking the STI course. You can do home study courses and come to the classroom on your night off. As a Marine veteran, you won't have to pay anything because it's covered by the VA."

Jim prevailed. I signed up and finished first in my class with a 98.4 grade average. My sales soared. My income jumped dramatically. More important, Jim taught me that learning never stops for the professional. *Profession* is defined as "a calling requiring specialized knowledge and often long and intensive academic preparation." I'd never thought of sales as a profession. Professionals were doctors, dentists, lawyers, CPAs, bankers, and airline pilots.

"Not only is sales a profession," said Jim, "but we're all selling something regardless of our calling." I started reading articles on sales. I bought books and tapes on sales. I attended sales seminars. I asked veteran salespeople for their advice. I was on the path to becoming a sales expert. I was naive to think success could be attained overnight without the help of others. The road to specialized knowledge is a process, a work in progress, a journey we can't make alone.

The challenge, of course, is to be more than a career student. Otherwise, your head is full of theories that are never used. To make learning more practical, you should understand these five steps of knowledge:

1. Awareness of General Information

The purpose of awareness is stimulation of thought. This is an exciting time of discovery. It's when you're exposed to a world of possibilities through learning. It's the difference between mere existence and a life of abundance.

When I was a kid, my mother made me *aware* of books, and I read constantly. Mom used to catch me reading books under the covers late at night with the aid of a flashlight. She forced me to go outside and play ball with the neighborhood kids because all I wanted to do was read.

2. Accumulation of General Information

The purpose of accumulation is to provide an educational foundation. You learn a little about a lot of things. These basic building blocks enable you to take learning to a higher level.

I did poorly in school my first nine years, but it wasn't due to a lack of reading. I just didn't apply myself in the classroom. I continued to read voraciously and *accumulated* a big base of *general information*. That served me well in the tenth, eleventh, and twelfth grades, when I finally got serious about my studies.

3. Repetition of Specialized Knowledge

The purpose of repetition is the comprehension of a select body of knowledge. It's how you become an authority in a particular field. The sheer volume of the information age makes it impossible to act on every idea. Specialization breaks down learning into manageable chunks. The art of mastery is often a gravitation toward a God-given talent or aptitude.

When a high school English teacher named Eloise Penn found out about my love of reading, she encouraged me to write book reports as a way to make learning more real. I fell in love with writing. Miss Penn thought I had a way with words and worked tirelessly with me on this *specialized knowledge*. The *repetition* of looking up words in the dictionary and thesaurus, diagramming sentences, editing, and endless rewriting were invaluable to me throughout high school and later in life.

4. Formation of Purpose Linked to Specialized Knowledge

The bridge between specialized knowledge and action is purpose. Learn all you can about your life's passion to help you discover why you are here. Expertise isn't enough. It has to be connected to a reason for living in order for you to use what you know in the most satisfying way.

After graduating from high school, I worked that summer as a sportswriting intern for the *Atlanta Constitution*. As I mentioned earlier, I spent a year writing for the Associated Press before going into sales. I always wanted to write for a living, but I had to make it work financially. I didn't link my specialized knowledge to a workable *purpose* until thirteen years later when I started my business.

5. Application of Specialized Knowledge

The purpose of application is to make a difference with your life. Practice daily what you know and love to do until you become an expert. A doer without knowledge is a fool. A career student without action is an intellectual. An intellectual without a purpose is lost. Specialized knowledge, purpose, and action are a winning combination.

Since my high school days and early journalistic training, I've *applied* my *specialized knowledge* in ways that have allowed me to earn a decent living doing what I love to do. I've written several books. I've written scripts for audio albums and content for seminar workbooks. I edit a newsletter. I write keynote speeches and deliver them to audiences across America and around the world. And it all started with an awareness of reading.

Thomas Macaulay, a nineteenth-century English historian, said, "Knowledge advances by steps, not by leaps." I first heard these words in high school and wondered how many steps would be necessary. Now, I understand the truth of Macaulay's statement because I've lived out these five steps over many years.

I'm especially grateful to Thelma Hall Askew, my mom, who helped me see the value of Step 1 in my childhood; to Miss Penn, who helped me see the value of Step 3 in high school; and to Jim Porterfield, who helped me see the value of Step 4 early in my sales career.

How are you doing with the steps of knowledge? Is your educational awareness as keen as it should be? Is there a piece of general information you can cultivate into specialized knowledge? Is your expertise a real passion? Do you need to do a better job of linking what you know to why you are here? Are you applying your specialized knowledge to something that's fun and exciting?

Remember, it's not just what you know, but how you use what you know that makes learning so rewarding. The application of specialized knowledge is truly an awesome power.

6

ABILITY VS. ATTITUDE

With competence and confidence, you're unstoppable! Ability enables you to perform competently. It's derived from God-given talent, aptitude, general information, specialized knowledge, and skills.

Attitude is your mental outlook on life. It's how you respond to the events of each day—negatively or positively. Without ability you're incompetent. Without a positive attitude, you lack the confidence to reach your full potential.

This lesson was burned indelibly into my memory one November day at Callaway Gardens, a resort in west Georgia. I'd run my first Peachtree Road Race on July 4, 1978—a distance of 6.2 miles down Atlanta's main thoroughfare. Brimming with competence and confidence, I decided to double the Peachtree distance by competing at Callaway a few months later.

The early miles of the race went well, and I felt fine. At mile nine I started to tire. At the ten-mile mark, my legs cramped. At mile eleven I wondered why anyone would do this to his body. By mile twelve some bad words came out of my mouth. At the end I questioned my sanity.

While waiting for a friend to complete the race, I noticed there were two finish lines—one for the 12.4-mile race and another for the marathon. About thirty minutes later, the winner of the 26.2-mile race crossed the finish line. My muscles ached after running a lot shorter distance. How could anyone endure twice the distance I'd run?

One marathoner really caught my eye. This man looked old enough to be my father. He was trim, fit, and breathing effortlessly after 26.2 miles. I felt ashamed. My thirty-three-year-old body was exhausted. I approached this man and asked, "First marathon, sir?" He replied, "No, it's my fourth one, and I feel better than ever." My shame turned to guilt, especially upon learning he was sixty-five years old.

I told him about my struggle to finish the shorter race and remarked, "Sir, I could never run a marathon." His reply was profound: "Young man, I know you have the physical ability to run 26.2 miles with the right training. If I can do it, you can do it. But as long as you have a mental barrier about the distance, you're right—you'll never run a marathon."

His words haunted me for weeks because he was right. I was thirty-two years younger than this man. I loved running. I had a physical gift for the sport. Despite these positives, I couldn't see myself running 26.2 miles. By the spring of 1979, I'd overcome this mental block and decided to train for my first marathon. A year after hearing this wise man's words, I finished the Callaway Gardens Marathon—the first of seven marathons in seven years.

Ability and the proper attitude are a dynamic duo. Never stop getting better at what you do, but beware of life's vexing attitude busters.

Attitude Buster #1: Problems

Problems are a part of life—people problems, work problems, family problems, money problems, health problems, and more. Failures complain about their problems and blame everyone else. Successful people become professional problem solvers and turn obstacles into opportunities.

I had a problem seeing myself run 26.2 miles. With the help of a stranger never seen again, a problem was converted into a possibility. What problems are keeping you from your optimum ability? Whom can you go to for help?

Attitude Buster #2: Self-pity

A self-pitying person allows a negative attitude to prevail by asking, "Why me?" A self-confident person lets a positive attitude triumph by asking, "How now?" Are you dwelling too much on *why* something occurred in the past? Or are you thinking more about *how* you'll face the future in spite of what's already happened?

That older marathoner didn't feel sorry for me. He issued a challenge to become all I could be. Are you holding pity parties or clinging to positive expectations?

Attitude Buster #3: Worry

Worriers tend to create anxiety about what could happen while endangering their present health through mental distress. Take the attitude you're too busy acting on today's tasks to worry unnecessarily about tomorrow's troubles. Many worries never come true, and even more are out of your control. Be concerned about the things you can change.

I could have worried for years about the drawbacks of running a marathon and missed out on developing my ability. What worries are holding you back from reaching your full potential? Choose work over worry, and watch your attitude soar.

Attitude Buster #4: Criticism

The word *criticize* has a negative connotation and rightly so. Some synonyms include *reprehend, condemn, censure,* and *denounce.* Do you want to be reprehended, condemned, censured, or denounced? I don't. Constructive criticism begins with what you did right, proceeds to suggestions for your improvement, and ends with a cheerful summary that gives you hope. In seeking feedback look for people who have your best interests at heart. Ignore critics offering cruel condemnation.

My marathon hero didn't condemn me for a negative comment. He offered positive reinforcement and hope. Are you surrounding yourself with people who bring you down or lift you up?

Attitude Buster #5: Fear of Failure

Your attitude helps determine how far you'll go in life. Did you know that most achievers have failed their way to success? Learn from your failures, but focus on your strengths and look to the future through a "can do" attitude.

I used that marathoner's success to turn my smaller achievement into a bigger one a year later. We fail only when we don't try. What fears are keeping you from maximizing your ability? How will you overcome your fears?

Often I speak at dental association conferences. The room is full of professionals with enormous ability. They've all graduated from college and dental school. They have other advanced training. They have prosperous practices. Yet no dentist could succeed with a negative attitude or poor chair-side manner.

What if your dentist greeted you like this? "Let's see, my anxious patient, you'll be getting a root canal today. I'm not going to administer any painkiller, though, because I'd like you to be as uncomfortable as possible. Are you ready to proceed?"

On the other hand, let's say you have a great attitude about getting in the ring with the heavyweight-boxing champion of the world. You shout, "Hey, buster, I'm going to do some damage to your ugly face today." But if you can't back up your threat with boxing skills, the fight will be over after one decent punch because attitude can carry you only so far.

There's no substitute for ability—it's an absolute given for success at anything. You should always be looking for ways to upgrade your competence. But no matter how talented you may be, a confident attitude will help you multiply your ability beyond your wildest imagination. I'm living proof.

Are life's attitude busters getting in the way of your ability? Are you like I was that first year at Callaway Gardens and think you can't? Or are you like that older marathon runner and think you can? If your attitude is good, what about your ability? Are you willing to go the distance with lifelong learning?

You can't succeed without ability. However, a positive attitude is the key to getting the most out of your talents. When ability and attitude work in concert, the lyrics of your life's song say, "I know . . . and I will!"

7

FACTS VS. FOCUS

Facts are pieces of information contributing to your knowledge, skills, and ability. In the information age, it's easy to become a facts junkie and an application flop. As Napoleon Hill said in *Think and Grow Rich*: "Knowledge is only potential power. It becomes power only when, and if, organized into definite plans of actions and directed towards a definite end."

Focus, or intense concentration, enables you to make wise use of what you know. Which is more important—facts or focus? Perhaps this embarrassing story will help you decide.

In 1981 Ron Creasy, Ron Varner, and yours truly founded the Chattahoochee Road Runners (CRR). Our club grew quickly. Within a year we staged our own road race, and it was a huge success. The inaugural CRR 10K (6.2 miles) attracted 600 runners, a record for a first-time race in Atlanta at that time.

The following year we met to plan our second race. As club president, I felt we could double the first year's attendance. "How are we going to draw 1,200 runners?" was the question everyone asked. I suggested a major corporate sponsor would give us marketing clout. The committee said, "Dick, you get the sponsor, and we'll support your idea."

I contacted Mike Daly, a club member and manager with Coca-Cola: "Mike, for the privilege of sponsoring the second annual CRR 10K, I need $5,000. Can I count on you?" I had a check two weeks later with instructions to use the funds for the promotion of a new product—Diet Coke. On race day, May 1, 1983, 1,200 runners stood at the starting line.

Mike and I were on a raised platform looking down at the horde of runners. I had fifteen seconds to greet everyone before the starting gun went off. A huge banner spanned the starting line. It read: "2nd Annual Chattahoochee Road Runners 10K." Beneath these words was the bright red Diet Coke logo.

"Good morning, runners," I said enthusiastically. "Welcome to the second annual CRR 10K. It's a thrill to see 1,200 runners, and we appreciate your support. Please help me give a big round of applause to Mike Daly and our sponsor . . . Diet Pepsi."

Those runners roared with laughter, but I didn't have a clue what I'd done until I felt the Coke manager coming up behind me. Placing his mouth on my ear like my old Marine drill instructor used to do, Mike bellowed, "It's Diet Coke, you idiot!"

Except for one word, that's an absolutely true story. You see, Mike Daly called me something a lot worse than *idiot,* but I'll leave that to your imagination. As the gun went off and the race began, I sensed I'd really messed up. "Mike, was it something I said?" He repeated my wayward words. I was so embarrassed. I apologized again and again, but the damage had been done. I knew the facts—Diet Coke. Unfortunately a lack of focus caused me to say the worst thing possible in front of 1,200 people.

The club members teased me about that incident for months, but it would be ten years later before the rest of the story could be told. In 1993 I wrote about the Diet Coke story in a publication. It got in the hands of a club member who was a Pepsi-Cola employee. His boss read the story and thought it was hilarious. He called to say, "Dick, I'd like to sponsor this year's club race under two conditions. I want you to be the guest starter of the race, and most important, you'd better be focused."

The second time around, I was focused. I'd learned from my awful mistake. It doesn't matter what you know if you don't use it properly. This requires razor-sharp focus, which comes from doing four things well:

1. Define your purpose.

2. Determine your dominant interests.

3. Develop your goals.

4. Decide on your priorities.

To do these four things well, please refer to The Master Plan Funnel Concept. Then check out the personal example, using four dominant intests and weekly goals. It provides a practical illustration for making this funnel work for you.

Here's the essence of this funnel: when priorities are done daily, goals are eventually realized. When goals are achieved in all of your dominant interests, there is balance. And when there is balance, you're more likely to fulfill your purpose and lead a more meaningful life.

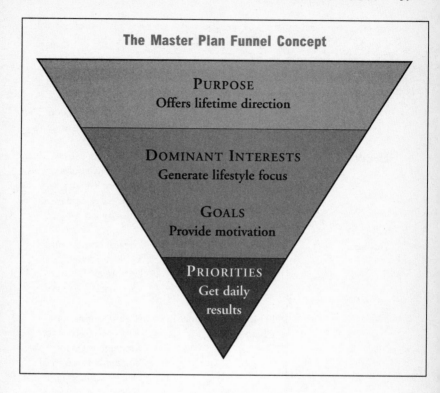

Purpose

I will strive "to do what is right" by maintaining integrity in all facets of my daily living. I will strive "to love mercy" by having a positive influence on others as a principle-centered role model and mentor. I will strive "to walk humbly with . . . God" through congruency between my beliefs and behavior.

DOMINANT INTERESTS	WEEKLY GOALS	DAILY PRIORITIES
Church	Teach Sunday school.	Prepare lesson on Tuesday night. Practice lesson on Thursday night. Deliver lesson on Sunday morning.
Health	Run twenty miles.	Do training runs of three to five miles on Monday, Tuesday, Wednesday, Friday, Saturday mornings.
Business	Deliver local keynote.	Practice keynote on Monday. Deliver keynote on Tuesday afternoon.
	Do half-day seminar in Chattanooga.	Review seminar on Wednesday. Drive to Chattanooga on Wednesday evening. Deliver seminar on Thursday morning. Return home on Thursday afternoon.
Family	Celebrate birthday of Tara, youngest stepdaughter.	Shop on Friday evening. Prepare for party on Saturday. Have party on Sunday afternoon.

If you're thinking, *Wow, this guy is really deliberate about his life,* you're right. However, it wasn't always this way. I've already told you about wasting a lot of time in my twenties and thirties and how it led to burnout. My life changed for the better once I learned to focus.

Focus means being on-purpose with a clearly defined statement of why you exist. Focus means carefully determining your dominant interests so you know where to spend your days. Focus means strategically developing your short-term and long-term goals to help you get where you want to go. And focus means prudently deciding on your priorities to get daily results.

You can't afford to waste time because there's so little of it. Be selective about what you learn because you won't live long enough to apply all you know. Don't settle for anything less than crystal-clear concentration, a lesson Coke manager Mike Daly taught me. And when you mess up, refocus and be prepared to take advantage of the next opportunity, as I did with Diet Pepsi ten years later.

Are the facts getting in the way of your focus? Could your focus be even sharper?

Start using The Master Plan Funnel Concept today, and take your life to new levels of success, happiness, and clarity. You're worth it.

8

VISION VS. GOALS

A vision is a general, idealistic view of where you'd like to go. For example, Dr. Martin Luther King Jr. painted a big picture of racial harmony with his "I Have a Dream" speech in 1963. He did not say, "I have a goal."

Goals are specific, realistic lists of what you intend to do on your life's journey. Dr. King didn't live to see his dream unfold. However, others have followed in his footsteps and turned the vision of this civil rights leader into a partial reality by implementing many goals.

Two other famous people—Dr. Norman Vincent Peale and Ruth Stafford Peale—helped me understand why specific goals should be preceded by a more general vision. In 1990 I met the Peales at the Atlanta airport and drove them downtown to the National Speakers Association convention. Dr. Peale was the closing speaker at ninety-two years of age.

"Sir," I said, "you've written numerous books, including *The Power of Positive Thinking*, a best-seller for years. You've spoken all over the world. Your *Guideposts* magazine has a huge circulation. No doubt you've probably saved some money. What I'm trying to say, Dr. Peale, is . . . you're not getting any younger. Why don't you retire?"

His answer reflected his lifetime vision: "I just plan to keep on keeping on. You know, Dick, there are still a few negative thinkers around!"

As we reached the convention hotel, a beaming bellman greeted us with these words: "Welcome to the Marriott Marquis. It's a great day to be alive, isn't it?" Dr. Peale shook hands with the bellman and replied, with a twinkle in his eye, "Young man, don't ever lose that smile. It's your greatest asset. And, yes, any day is a great day to be alive when you're ninety-two."

In that short moment of truth, Norman Vincent Peale showed why he had such a vibrant vision for a world of positive thinkers. He demonstrated his vision to that bellman through a radiant face, kind words, and a keen sense of humor. This congruent behavior was a reflection of his vision and long-term goals to make the world a better place to live.

Dr. Peale died at ninety-five. Three years later, Mrs. Peale invited me to Pawling, New York, to speak to her leadership team. In the lobby of the Peale Center for Christian Living, I noticed a life-sized bronze statue of Norman Vincent Peale. It reminded me of the short man with a giant vision—one that continues to influence people all over the world through his books, articles, legacy, and organization.

Mrs. Peale invited me to her office prior to my presentation. She had just celebrated her ninetieth birthday with the unveiling of her late husband's statue. She was dressed in a business suit and looked terrific. At an age most people will never see, Mrs. Peale was still carrying on Dr. Peale's positive thinking vision.

As we talked, it became evident why the Peale vision is so powerful. Mrs. Peale is focused on the future instead of resting on the feats of her famous husband. I listened intently as this remarkable lady shared her long-term goals for the Peale Center at ninety years of age!

She wanted to expand the prayer ministry through the Internet, toll-free telephone, and fax. She wanted to develop a positive thinking program for use in businesses. She wanted to expand the School of Practical Christianity. She wanted to launch additional magazines.

Mrs. Peale continued: "Many people my age—and lots of younger people, too—have slipped into the habit of negative thinking. They feel discouraged, depressed, lonely, and fearful. The fact is they don't have to be. What is sometimes astonishing to me is that the principles for positive living Norman first popularized are as valid today as they were fifty years ago. And we are going to show people how to put those principles to work."

According to Dr. Peale, "The positive principle never thinks in past terms but always thinks future." By their very nature, visions and goals are about the future. When her husband died, Mrs. Peale replied to my sympathy card with a witty letter focused primarily on the future: "Norman is probably gathering all the angels together and making a speech. Now we all have work to do . . . our task is to blanket the world [read: vision] with *The Power of Positive Thinking*. We have a plan [read: goals] to do just that."

If visions and goals are good enough for Dr. King and the Peales, they're good enough for me and should be good enough for you. My vision is to "help people do a better job of balancing the work they need with the lives they lead." To help live my dreams, I set short-term and long-term goals using the following "7 Rs" system.

1. Respectable

If your goals aren't aligned with the high standards of your purpose statement (see Chapter 2), why pursue them? You'll be out of balance and lacking congruency.

I started running in 1964 to get ready for Marine Corps boot camp. After years of physical fitness, it would be inconsistent with my life's purpose to set goals that abuse my body. As a result, I have no desire to smoke, use drugs, drink alcohol, etc.

2. Realistic

I'm an advocate of thinking big, but your goals need to be tempered with reality and patience. Set yourself up to succeed by pursuing fewer, realistic goals. As you gain confidence and momentum, go after loftier ambitions.

If you've never run before, you wouldn't start by entering a marathon. You'd walk a short distance your first day. As your endurance grew, you'd increase your distance gradually and mix in some running with walking. As your fitness improved over several months, you'd run a series of shorter races leading up to the marathon distance of 26.2 miles.

3. Record

Written goals provide better accountability. A dream is a good starting point, but the process of turning your vision into goals becomes more pinpointed through the written word. Many studies prove why success increases when goals are put on paper.

For example, I write down my running goals at the start of each year. I've kept a running log since 1980. If one of my goals is to run one thousand miles for the year, I have a daily record of my progress. At the end of the week, I can see if I'm on schedule. By year's end I know if I've succeeded.

4. Reduce to the Specific

Don't say, "I want to move up in my company." Be specific and say, "I want to be vice president of marketing by June 1 of a certain year, and here's how I plan to do it."

The difference between a vision and a goal is a deadline and sense of urgency. If you're serious about turning your goals into reality, be specific.

When I was running marathons, I set my goals every December for the following year—date of the race, exact marathon, a detailed training program, and so on. Nothing was left to chance.

5. Reflect Upon Them Often

Visualize the attainment of your goals to provide constant reinforcement and maintain the intensity of your focus. Subconsciously you see yourself succeeding or failing. Which is it?

In Chapter 6 I told you how a marathoner old enough to be my father taught me a crucial lesson about visualization. When you remove the mental barriers, your road to success is easier, clearer, and likelier.

6. Relentlessly Pursue

How many people have failed to accomplish a goal when the end was around the next bend? How many people have achieved a goal on sheer stubbornness? Nothing happens without effort, so go for your goals with gusto.

My seventh and last marathon was a personal best, but it required a relentless effort due to circumstances beyond my control. I had trained harder than ever. However, on race day it was sixteen degrees with a twenty-mile-an-hour head wind most of the way. I wanted to quit several times. Thanks to a friend and my wife, who accompanied me the final three miles, I persisted and finished in three hours, nineteen minutes, forty-seven seconds.

7. Responsibility

No matter how goal-driven you are, life is unpredictable. There may be times when you'll have to postpone your goals due to the death of loved ones, health problems, business hardships, financial difficulties, and more. The right thing to do is to deal with these trials. When the time is right, resume the quest of your goals, or reassess what you want out of life.

I finally gave up marathons in 1986 when the demands of operating a business, being a husband, raising two stepdaughters, and serving my professional association and church pushed me to the brink of burnout for a second time. Scaling back my exercise was the responsible thing to do, and I've never regretted this decision.

What is your life's vision? Is it as clear as the dreams of Martin Luther King Jr. and the Peales? What are your short-term and long-term goals? Short-term goals can be daily, weekly, monthly, quarterly, or annual. Long-term goals are beyond a year. Set goals within each of your dominant interests (see Chapter 3), be more balanced, and burn brightly.

Let the power of goal-setting take you to a greater level of self-motivation. Let the joy of goal-getting allow you to do what you love and love what you do.

9

PLANS VS. PRIORITIES

A plan is an intention. It's passive. The blueprints are drawn, but the work hasn't begun.

A priority is a plan whose time has come. It's active. The notion is set in motion when it becomes of leading importance.

On February 25, 1999, Dick Dillon had just read one of my books and planned to hire me as speaker at his company. "When I return from this trip," he told his secretary prior to heading for the Atlanta airport, "remind me to call Dick Biggs." It was a plan, not a priority.

On the same day, I was heading to the Atlanta airport for a flight to North Carolina. As I pulled into the remote parking lot, an attendant said, "Sir, it's your lucky day. We have only one parking space left, and it's yours." He handed me a ticket and pointed to the last spot. I couldn't pull into my space because it was blocked by an open door from the car that got the next to last parking place. I waited patiently as a man and woman unloaded several pieces of luggage.

Finally the gentleman realized what was happening, shut his door, and apologized. "No problem," I said. "I'm in no hurry." I'd arrived early because I had more luggage than usual. Besides my regular two bags, I had a large box with "Biggs" written all over it. My client had called at the last minute requesting more books, which meant they'd have to go with me on the flight. I lugged this heavy box to the airport shuttle van and returned for my two bags.

When I reentered the van, a voice said, "You're Dick Biggs, aren't you?" It was the gentleman who had blocked my parking spot. He smiled, shook my hand, and said, "I'm Dick Dillon, and this is Linda, my wife. I'm with Lucent Technologies. I saw your name on that box and recognized you from a picture in one of your books. Believe it or not, you're on my list of people to call when I get back from this trip. I'd like you to speak to our company. Here's my business card."

The following week, Dick Dillon turned his plan into a priority when he chose a date for my presentation. He invited other Lucent managers to this session, including Julie Onstott. During my balanced living seminar, I referred briefly to my new mentor program. I didn't know it at the time, but Julie was thinking about a mentor program at Lucent. It was a plan, not a priority. Over the next few months, we worked out the details for launching such a program.

On June 2, 2000, Julie's plan became a priority when Lucent purchased the rights to *Maximize Your Moments With The Masters*. This comprehensive mentor program includes an orientation session, twelve monthly seminars, four quarterly evaluations, and a closing celebration. Each protégé and mentor receives a customized workbook, companion reading guide, audio album, and e-mail access to me throughout the program. It was a big investment for Lucent and a major opportunity for me.

Dick Dillon says it was divine intervention that caused us to meet on that airport shuttle van. After all, we arrived at the airport parking lot within seconds of each other. We got the last two parking spots next to each other in a lot with several hundred spaces. And if my North Carolina client hadn't called late asking for more books, there would have been no box with "Biggs" written all over it.

Julie Onstott believes it was a miracle. I was there to talk about another topic, yet managed to say the right words at the right time to the right person about the right topic. Frankly I agree with Julie. And even if you think it was sheer luck, one thing is certain—these Lucent managers turned their plans into priorities as a result of our association.

Dick Dillon and Julie Onstott understand prioritization, which is the ranking of your goals in the order of importance. It's the catalyst that sparks daily results and produces long-term success. That's why priorities form the tip of The Master Plan Funnel Concept (Chapter 7). This filtering system allows you to act daily on the most important things in your career and personal life.

Use this "5 Ds" system to help you prioritize your goals, get more done, and live the life you've imagined:

I. Determine the Importance

Make sure a priority is just that, or you'll be busy and unproductive. Develop the habit of listing the things that *must* be done today in the order of importance, then do your best to stay focused. Always ask: *What is the most important thing I should be doing right now?*

For example, I thought my first book was a priority in the late 1980s, but other matters seemed to get in the way of my best intentions. This "priority" lingered for several years because my plan was unclear and poorly conceived. It's difficult to turn a plan into a priority when you don't know where you're going. The situation changed when I had a clear picture of the book framework, chapter titles, and writing format.

2. Deadline It

When you're developing your priorities each evening for the next day, assign each activity a specific time slot. List the priorities for every dominant interest of your life. Check off priorities as you achieve them. Set new deadlines for remaining or new priorities. Never forget that a priority gets preference over anything else.

In the summer of 1992, I finally assigned a deadline for the completion of my book. I developed a strict schedule for the next six months. I wrote for three months. I got feedback for a month. I rewrote for two months. A time line turned wishful thinking into a priority.

3. Decide on a Plan of Implementation

Once a goal has been prioritized and assigned a deadline, decide on the best way to get the job done. Planning saves time, but it can also be a deadly time-waster. Beware of the dreaded disease known as "paralysis from analysis" by planning your work (passive), then working your plan (active).

My first book called for one hundred, two-page chapters centered on four key principles. The plan was to write twenty-five "essays" every three weeks in June, July, and August. If I produced eight or nine short chapters each week—or approximately two a day over a five-day week—my plan would be implemented. Sure enough, I finished on time because I prioritized the plan daily.

4. Delegate if Possible

Patricia Fripp, a speaker friend, says, "There's no point doing well that which you shouldn't be doing at all." If possible, assign people with different skills to handle what you don't do well. You'll be more productive and pleased, and so will the people around you.

When it was time to edit, I was too close to my work to be objective. My wife and three friends read the manuscript utilizing their unique skills. One read it for overall flow. Another read it for spelling and grammar. Another read it for content. And another read it for accuracy. With these suggestions in hand a month later, I devoted two months to rewriting. Proper delegation and teamwork improve any project, and my book was no exception.

5. Do It!

Nike's "Just Do It" promotional campaign was one of the most successful in American business history. This simple but profound message said it all: while dreaming and planning are important, there's no substitute for action. Knowing makes you smart, but doing sets you apart.

In July 1993, I received an advance copy of *If Life Is a Balancing Act, Why Am I So Darn Clumsy?* This book is in its third printing and is a terrific marketing tool. People often say to me after a program, "Dick, one of these days I'm going to find the time to write a book." My advice: when your book—or anything else in life—becomes a priority, you'll make the time. Just do it.

Life is about choices, and choosing is about prioritizing. Choose wisely each day and keep fine-tuning throughout your life until you get the results you want. If what you're doing right now isn't your most important priority, you're wasting time. Hey, I squandered a handful of years believing my book was a priority when it was merely a plan. I learned it is important to make each day count.

Lucent managers Dick Dillon (retired) and Julie Onstott taught me a valuable lesson about turning plans into priorities. What about you? Are you willing to use the "5 Ds" system to get more daily results? What choices are you making for a more fulfilling life?

Nothing will produce more long-term results than daily prioritization. It's the difference between conceiving and achieving. Prioritize habitually, and watch your plans become your destiny and legacy.

10

MOTIVATION VS. INSPIRATION

Motivation is about doing. It means you have the inner drive and physical energy to make something happen. There's good reason for the term *self-motivation.*

Inspiration is about thinking. It's how you're stimulated mentally by external forces.

You simply can't do your best thinking or be inspired at the highest level without tapping into the wisdom of the ages.

As a rule, self-motivation is a by-product of inspiration based on your choice of external influences—family, friends, business, place of worship, community, media, government, books, Internet, and countless other sources. The exception, of course, is motivation by force and fear when a situation is out of your control.

When I was a kid, my father motivated by force when he spanked me—a situation out of my control. My mother motivated by fear when she threatened to ground me—a situation out of my control. When I joined the Marines at age nineteen, I discovered a deeper level of motivation by force and fear—a situation out of my control.

It happened rather innocently one day when I dropped out of college. I visited Pete Jaynes, a good friend and neighbor who had just graduated from high school. Pete was an excellent student and college material. To my surprise, Pete had joined the Marines. That was hard to accept since I'd played quarterback and safety on the football team, and Pete was our water boy.

Not to be outdone, I joined the Marines the next day and returned proudly to show Pete my papers and serial number—#2110713. Smiling wryly, Pete said, "I hate to tell you this, Dick, but I really didn't join the Marines." Well, Pete joined the Marines the following day because I took him down to the recruiting station. That's why his serial number is eleven digits behind mine—#2110724.

On October 20, 1964, Pete and I rode the bus to Parris Island, South Carolina, for three months of boot camp and some serious motivation by force and fear. We arrived late at night and were greeted by a screaming behemoth. He was our senior drill instructor, or DI. Tall, lean, muscular, and tan, Staff Sergeant McClain had a gravelly voice and wore a brown Smokey Bear hat atop his crewcut.

As we lined up in a makeshift military formation, our DI roared: "I can't believe they sent me such a scuzzy bunch of civilian scumbags to make Marines out of in twelve weeks. Why, you look like a herd of sheep milling around out there. But I'll tell you one thing, sweet-hearts, you'd better give your souls to God because the rest of you is mine." Actually Sergeant McClain said it a little differently from that, but you'd better believe we were highly motivated by force and fear for the next three months because things were out of our control.

There's one entrance into Parris Island, and it's guarded twenty-four hours a day. We were surrounded by the Atlantic Ocean, high tides, sharks, dangerous marshes, and snake-infested swamps. If any-one refused to cooperate, there was STB—Special Training Branch, a notorious place reserved for unmotivated recruits. After STB reformed a recruit, his reward was a new platoon and the agony of starting boot camp all over again. Thankfully I never visited STB, and I graduated on time.

Of course, in the civilian world, motivation by force and fear doesn't work too well. You can always leave a job or an unhappy situation. I had no way of getting off Parris Island without risking my life or suffering serious disciplinary action. We received twelve weeks of Marine-style motivation because that's what it took to get us ready for combat. We didn't have any choice, and Sergeant McClain reminded us of that daily: "There's the right way, the wrong way, and the Marine Corps way." In retrospect I wouldn't trade this training for anything because it taught me the importance of good habits, hard work, and teamwork.

I'm also grateful for parents who were more concerned about my self-discipline than my self-esteem. Children need a certain amount of motivation by force and fear (tough love) balanced with a caring, nurturing environment (gentle love). Between strict parents and Marine Corps boot camp, I was prepared for the challenging transition from boyhood to manhood.

Adult motivation is different. You're responsible for your own motivation through the inspiration of your choice. If your boss is acting like a Marine DI, you can find a new supervisor or another company. If a client or supplier is acting like a Marine DI, you can ask this person to change or do business with someone else. If a stockholder is acting like a Marine DI, you can tell him to settle down or invest his money elsewhere.

It comes down to this truth: to gain a greater *quantity* of self-motivation, surround yourself with the greatest *quality* of inspiration.

Here are six ways to better inspiration and, in turn, greater self-motivation:

1. Read from a good book
at least fifteen minutes every day.

If you're too busy to read for this minimal amount of time each day, could you be too busy? Be selective, consistent, and don't try to keep up with all the reading you'd like to do. Look for nuggets of wisdom. If you can read for an hour a day, you can become proficient on most any topic within a year.

As speaker Charlie "Tremendous" Jones likes to say: "You'll be the same in five years as you are today except for the people you meet and the books you read." My favorite book is the Bible. It isn't called the *motivated Word of God,* because the Bible can't make you do anything. It's known as the *inspired Word of God* for good reason. When you discover the inspirational truths of the Bible, you want to do as it says.

2. Listen to educational,
upbeat audiotapes or CDs each week.

The beauty about this form of inspiration is that you can learn while driving, flying, or exercising. Tapes and CDs are excellent reinforcement tools. As you listen to these messages again and again, your subconscious mind is recording these impressions to be used later in ways you can't imagine. First, I listen to the message. Second, I relisten and take notes. Third, I write down action ideas.

3. Belong to an accountability group that meets at least monthly.

My group meets weekly, but no one makes every meeting. A group of four to eight people is ideal. We talk about everything from our spiritual lives, families, and communities, to our careers, problems, and concerns for others. Confidentiality is crucial for building trust and rapport. In today's "I have a right to do whatever I want" society, it's important to understand we're accountable to ourselves, others, and God.

4. Attend at least one worthwhile seminar every quarter.

Perhaps nothing is as inspirational as a live presentation given by a polished, proficient seminar leader. When you hear something you already know, ask, *What am I doing about it?* Instead of returning with pages of notes that collect dust on your desk, focus on one or two ideas you can put into practice immediately. Speaker Terry Paulson recommends a "keepers worth keeping" notebook that you review regularly.

5. Join a mastermind group that meets at least semiannually.

Earlier in my career, I belonged to a mastermind group of eight speakers who spoke on different topics. The idea came from *Think and Grow Rich*, a best-selling book by Napoleon Hill. We provided encouragement and support. We shared ideas. We offered feedback. It was amazing to watch seven peers take one of my mediocre ideas and turn it into a great one. If you want to accelerate your learning curve,

I highly recommend a mastermind group that meets at least twice a year, preferably in a quiet retreat setting.

6. Write a review of your life every year.

I've been writing annual reviews since 1974. Between Christmas and New Year, I sit in front of a roaring fireplace with a legal pad and reflect on the highlights of the past twelve months. I usually end up with seven or eight pages covering all areas of my life. This exercise serves a dual purpose. If it has been a difficult year, I look to the future with hope and inspiration. And if it has been an exciting year, I thank God for my blessings.

I receive many calls from employers who want more motivated employees. I always ask these callers how long they want their people to be motivated after my presentation. The usual answer is, "Every day." My response: "Okay, let's see if I've got this straight. You want me to be the motivator, and after I'm gone, you want your employees to be motivated every day. Are you prepared to hire me every day for the next year?" The typical reply is, "All right, Dick, I see what you mean."

A great motivational speech can generate an incredible short-term high, but it's unlikely to produce long-term motivation among the troops. People need more than momentary motivation. They need ongoing inspiration through proven, practical programs of professional development and personal growth. The Merriam Webster Dictionary defines "inspirer" as simply the catalyst or "agent that provokes or speeds significant behavioral change or action." It's up to you to turn inspiration into motivation.

What are you doing to take your inspiration to the next level? Are you reading regularly? Are you listening to educational tapes while you're driving to work? Are you attending worthwhile seminars? Have you considered an accountability or a mastermind group? Will you start writing a review of each year? What are some other ways you can increase your inner drive and productivity?

It has been many years since I was disciplined by my parents or had a Marine DI in my face, yet I'm highly motivated through the inspiration of my choosing. I'm hoping you'll choose the right sources of inspiration, for they will determine your degree of self-motivation and level of mastery.

11

PROCRASTINATION VS. DECISIVENESS

Procrastination is the subtle art of sabotaging your potential. The procrastinator is caught in the twilight zone between "I'm going to" and "I did." The result is overanalyzing and underachieving.

Decisiveness is your will to overcome the greatest gap in life—the one between knowing and doing. Call it the procrastination gap. The decisive person has the courage to make difficult choices and the discipline to act.

Jack McDowell is an amazing example of a life that was changed because decisiveness triumphed over procrastination. Jack is a good friend, one of my mentors and the most decisive person I know. But if Clem Plattner had procrastinated one snowy day in Minnesota, Jack's life might not have turned out so well. Here's the story in Jack's own words:

When I was 12, I joined the 4-H Club in our town of 240 people in the northern woods of Minnesota. When I was 14, I entered a public speaking contest sponsored by the Minnesota 4-H Clubs. I was very shy, but my parents encouraged me to enter this contest to help overcome my fear of people. I memorized my five-minute speech and presented it twice a day for a month to our cows as I milked them. Those cows were my first audience.

The contest was held on a Saturday in the school gymnasium. There were only six contestants, and I was the youngest. Most were seniors from other schools in the county. Much to my surprise, I won the contest and an opportunity to participate in the district contest.

My phone rang a few days later. The caller was Clem Plattner. He asked my mom if he could come to the farm, take my picture and write a story for the county newspaper about my contest victory. Mom told him we'd been snowed in for several days and that he'd have to walk a mile through very deep snow from the front gate to our home.

Two days later, Clem Plattner walked that mile through the deep snow to take my picture and write a story about my speech. Mr. Plattner told my parents he wanted to show the people of Minnesota what a young farm boy in Cass County could accomplish—a boy who some years later would present a gold 4-H paperweight to President Harry Truman, which he kept on his desk until he retired from office.

Through his genuine encouragement and the promotion of my work on behalf of the 4-H organization, Clem Plattner introduced me to my first understanding of what I was able to accomplish. He inspired me to develop the ability to think on my feet. Years later, I was the keynote speaker at the Republican State Convention and was offered the chairmanship of the National Youth for Eisenhower when he first ran for president.

When you understand where I came from and how far I've been able to go, you begin to realize how much Clem Plattner meant to my life. He told me over and over that I could accomplish whatever I set my mind to if I was willing to make the sacrifices necessary to achieve the results I sought.

It has been 58 years since Clem Plattner came into my life. As I look back, I can see that 14-year-old boy delivering his five-minute speech to the cows as he milked them twice a day. I can see him addressing the rows of corn as he cultivated the field prior to addressing the Republican State Convention in Minnesota. I can see him standing beside a former president telling the audience how a first-time voter felt about his country. I can see Clem Plattner walking through deep snow to a farmhouse to take a picture of a boy who had won a speaking contest.

I shall never cease to be thankful for my first mentor. My daily commitment is to do all I possibly can to encourage those with whom I come in contact to achieve all they are capable of doing. It is my conviction that the only way we can serve our God is to serve his people.

To fully appreciate Jack's story, you need to know the rest of it. He was the only child of a successful California contractor. Jack's youth included prestigious schools, a German nanny, and exploits displaying his potential. His lifestyle changed abruptly when his father's illness led the family to an abandoned farm in northern Minnesota.

At age twelve Jack assumed the man-sized challenge of working on a farm, supporting the family, and pursuing a high school education.

He worked seven days a week, rising two hours past midnight to study for three hours and perform farm duties until 10:30 each night. Jack graduated with honors despite attending high school classes for less than one full school year.

A disease infected the registered dairy cattle the McDowells had bred and raised so carefully. The herd had to be slaughtered. The family, already burdened with heavy medical bills, was forced to sell everything but the land to raise enough money to subsist for the next several years. The local banker loaned Jack enough money to buy a car and provided three hundred dollars to live on until he found an employer.

Jack drove to Dallas to seek an interview with H. L. Hunt, the oil tycoon. The young man sold Mr. Hunt on defending free enterprise in the high schools. Hunt offered to sponsor Jack's idea for one year provided he agreed to assist with a fund-raising effort for The Salvation Army in Jonesboro, Arkansas. Upon completing that project, Jack was asked to lead another campaign, and the rest is history.

Jack conducted more than 100 successful capital campaigns in his career, including 78 for The Salvation Army. His average campaign reached an amazing 169 percent of quota. He has raised more money for The Salvation Army than anyone in the world. McDowell retired in 1992, but he remains active in the affairs of The Salvation Army and has established a fund to help train future officers. He's the author of *The Power of Purpose: Your Pathway to Dynamic Living, Wealth & Personal Success.*

The next time you're tempted to procrastinate, think about what's at stake. Do you have the bad habit of making any of the following excuses?

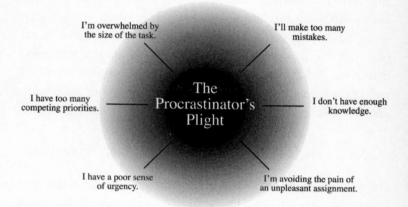

I'm overwhelmed by
the size of the task.

I'll make too many
mistakes.

I have too many
competing priorities.

The
Procrastinator's
Plight

I don't have enough
knowledge.

I have a poor sense
of urgency.

I'm avoiding the pain of
an unpleasant assignment.

You can't eliminate procrastination—hey, you're human—but you can decrease it by observing this five-point model for greater decisiveness:

1. Give careful consideration to all the facts and options.

This is the logical part of any decision. Gather all the pertinent information and weigh your choices. George Moore was right when he said in *The Bending of the Bough*: "The difficulty in life is the choice." When you face complex decisions, seek out the advice of more experienced people. Do your homework, and don't be overcome by fear.

2. Pay attention to your heart, intuition, and gut feeling.

This is the emotional part of any decision. If something makes sense but doesn't feel right, beware. For example, get-rich schemes seem so logical. Yet you know in your heart that if something seems too good to be true, it probably is. My wife's intuition is always better than mine because I'm more logical in nature. Over the years Judy and I have used our individual strengths to help us become a better decision-making team.

3. Don't second-guess yourself once you make a decision.

You make too many important decisions in life to waste valuable time ruing past choices. It's easy to say, "Golly, I knew that was the wrong thing to do," or "Gee, I had a feeling it wouldn't work out," or "Gosh, I should have waited a little longer before . . ."

Do your research (Step 1), listen to your heart (Step 2), and then have the courage to act and accept the consequences of your results.

4. Believe you'll probably make more good choices than bad ones in a lifetime.

Richard Pryor, a comedian known for his graphic language, once offered this wise advice: "You don't get old being no fool." As we age, we should also get smarter. Learn from your poor decisions in the early years. Celebrate your good choices as you mature. When your life is at an end, the odds are in your favor that you will have made more good choices than bad ones.

5. Anticipate success, but don't be afraid to fail.

Sir Winston Churchill said many profound things, but here's my favorite quote from this great English leader: "Success is going from failure to failure without loss of enthusiasm." That's the story of my life. What I've learned to do is to ask these critical questions when making difficult decisions:

- What will happen if I don't act?

- What are the possibilities if I do act?

- If for some reason I don't succeed, what's the worst thing that could happen, and can I deal with the consequences?

Are you procrastinating unnecessarily? If so, what are you willing to do about this problem? Will you use the five-point model for greater decisiveness in the next thirty days? Do you need to post the critical questions listed above on your computer or calendar as a daily reminder to be a better decision maker?

Procrastination is public enemy number one of achievement. Choose wisely by considering all the facts and options, paying attention to your heart, eliminating the second-guess mentality, learning from your bad decisions, and not being afraid to fail. Your reward will be peak performance balanced with more purposeful living.

Jack McDowell fulfilled his vast potential because he chose action over inaction. Clem Plattner would be so proud of his protégé. And you'll be proud of yourself when you minimize procrastination by maximizing decisiveness.

12

BURNOUT VS. ENTHUSIASM

Burnout is the extinguishing of your spiritual, mental, physical, or emotional enthusiasm. It happens when a single dominant interest becomes your life. For example, a workaholic is often worn out by excessive enthusiasm. Or burnout happens when you make too many commitments among your dominant interests and your circuits become overloaded.

Enthusiasm is derived from the Greek word *enthousiasmos,* which means "to be filled with spirit." A spirited person wakes up each day and says, "Good morning, God." A burned-out person moans, "Good God, morning." The challenge is to be balanced enough to maintain your enthusiasm without burning out.

Jim Fixx struggled with this delicate balancing act for many years. In his mid-thirties Fixx was obese. He was a heavy smoker. He had poor eating habits. He had a cholesterol count of 250. He never exercised. And he was a burned-out man.

One day while playing tennis, Fixx strained his right calf and took up running to strengthen his legs. He quit smoking. He changed his eating habits and lost weight.

He worked his way up to running seventy miles per week. He went from burnout to burning very brightly.

In 1977 Fixx wrote *The Complete Book of Running* followed by *The Second Book of Running* a year later. These best-sellers, coupled with Frank Shorter's Olympic marathon victory in 1972 and the publication of *Aerobics* by Dr. Ken Cooper in 1968, paved the way for the fitness boom in America. If the Fixx name is starting to jog your memory (groan), you may remember that, at age fifty-two, he dropped dead of a heart attack while running. How could such a fit man be so unhealthy?

Dr. Cooper addressed that question when he wrote *Running Without Fear.*[1] The autopsy of Fixx revealed the heart of an unhealthy man. He had severe blockage of his coronary arteries, scar tissue indicating at least three minor heart attacks before the one that killed him, and an unusually enlarged heart. He also had the number one risk factor of heart disease—family history and heredity. His father suffered two heart attacks, and the second was fatal when he was forty-three.

In addition Fixx was under a lot of stress. He had been divorced twice, changed jobs a lot, and suffered a $50,000 investment loss. He disliked travel, interviews, and public speaking but was forced into these activities due to the popularity of his books. Ironically Fixx was at the famed Cooper Clinic in Dallas six months prior to his death and declined a stress test that could have saved his life. Dr. Cooper agreed with the Vermont medical examiner that "running did not cause [his] death . . . severe and silent coronary arteriosclerosis did."

While it's true that physical fitness can do wonders for your energy, productivity, and longevity, it's just one of the components of a healthy lifestyle. Like anything else in life, too much of a good thing can sabotage the precarious balance between burnout and enthusiasm. Dr. Cooper warns, "People at all levels of fitness may have a tendency to overdo it. Given his underlying coronary problems, Jim Fixx overdid it."

You can't do your best if you don't feel your best. That's why overall good health is so critical to your peak performance. To lessen your risk of burnout, optimize your enthusiasm, and increase your chances for a healthier life, practice these Eight Elite Enhancers of Longer Life:

1. Get the proper amount of sleep and relaxation.

Are you working too many hours at one career? Do you have multiple jobs? Are you too committed in other areas of your life? If so, you're probably not getting enough rest and recovery time. The price tag could be burnout, sickness, disease, or premature death.

Dr. Cooper believes "Jim Fixx was exhausted" when he checked into his hotel on July 20, 1984—the day of his death. There's no doubt he was stressed out. Sleep is the body's way of restoring energy. Most people require six to eight hours of sleep per night. You also need to plan specific times of stress relief, which will be discussed in Chapter 17.

2. Have regular, complete, preventive medical and dental examinations.

A man complained about the price of a complete physical exam when told there was nothing wrong with him. Did he want to learn he had cancer to get his money's worth? Preventive health care is a lot less costly than the treatment of sickness and disease.

See your dentist at least semiannually. Make sure your annual medical exams include cancer screening and stress testing. It's a small price to pay for peace of mind. If something is wrong, early detection can be a lifesaver.

How much do you think Jim Fixx would pay for a thorough physical exam if he were alive today? A properly administered and interpreted stress test can detect blockage of the arteries. After more than forty years at his clinic, Dr. Cooper cites numerous case histories of lives that have been saved due to stress testing. Of Fixx, Dr. Cooper concludes: "There's no question in my mind that his heart abnormalities would have been detected—and probably saved his life."

3. Eat a balanced, sensible diet, and maintain the proper weight.

You don't have to live on lettuce, soup, mangos, and kumquats. I sure don't. A balanced, sensible diet means eating some of all of the food groups each day. Just eat more whole grains, fruits, vegetables, fish, and poultry than red meats, starches, dairy products, and desserts. Drink a lot of water. And if you're overweight, don't blame it on metabolism. Obese people have a higher metabolic rate than skinny people due to more muscle tissue.

According to Dr. Cooper, Fixx ate a lot of steak, potatoes, shrimp, lobster, and other rich foods before his lifestyle change. When he switched to more grilled fish, salads, carbohydrates, vegetables, fruits, and cereal, his weight went from 215 to 160 pounds. Taped to my computer is this simple reminder from *Bits & Pieces*: The Five-Word Weight Loss Formula: Eat Less and Exercise More.

4. Exercise aerobically, reasonably, and consistently.

The rare person can maintain the proper weight through diet only. Crash diets don't produce long-term results for most people because they revert to their old eating habits after attaining a certain weight loss. Aerobic (the word means "with oxygen") exercises such as walking, hiking, running, swimming, rowing, and biking will help you burn more calories and lose weight. In addition your lungs will process more air with less effort, your heart will grow stronger and pump more blood with fewer strokes, and you'll develop more stamina.

Fixx didn't need to run seventy miles a week to be fit. Dr. Cooper says you can acquire a reasonable level of aerobic fitness by exercising twenty minutes a day, four times per week. The idea is to train at 65 to 80 percent of your maximum heart rate (maximum is 220 for most people). Of course, consistency is the key to better fitness and proper weight control. Check with your doctor before starting an aerobic exercise program.

5. Avoid all tobacco products.

I knew a man who died in his late fifties in need of a heart transplant. He wouldn't stop smoking and was ineligible for the heart waiting list. Cigarette smoking accounts for one-fifth of all deaths in America. The passive fumes endanger nonsmokers. An average smoker loses a day of the future for every eight days he or she smokes. While this bad habit has cost America billions of dollars in health care costs, the tobacco companies have repeatedly denied the dangers of their product.

Fixx had the courage to stop smoking, and that change probably prolonged his life. He lived nine years longer than his father had but still died at fifty-two. If you smoke, think about some of the chemicals emitted from a burning cigarette. Benzine is a flammable liquid used in making dyes and rubber. Carbon monoxide is a poisonous oxygen blocker, and the same one ejected from your vehicle exhaust pipe. Formaldehyde is a disinfectant and preservative. Ammonia is a poisonous gas used in making fertilizers and explosives. Hydrogen cyanide is a poisonous rat killer.

6. Avoid drugs, and use alcohol in moderation, if at all.

Illegal drug use is just stupid. If you're one of those people who can drink alcohol in moderation, fine, but please don't do it while driving. Excessive drinking is expensive, damages the liver and brain, alters behavior, and sets a poor example for the people around you. Perhaps the greatest danger is the regret you could suffer later in life. Mickey Mantle, a Hall of Fame baseball player who had a liver transplant, pleaded in a television commercial before his death, "Don't be like me."

Dr. Cooper reports that Fixx drank "a few glasses of wine" with his meals. While some studies claim moderate wine drinking can actually be good for your heart, Dr. Cooper maintains "there's no evidence that moderate alcohol consumption gives us the same long-term health benefits as does exercise." I've never used drugs, but I drank alcoholic beverages without moderation for eighteen years. I gave up this addiction in 1984 and haven't missed it a bit.

7. Use home smoke detectors, and wear vehicle seat belts.

Why would you fail to install these life-saving devices in your home when the cost is so affordable? As for vehicle seat belts, I've heard people say, "I don't wear them because they're uncomfortable." If you really want to be uncomfortable, try slamming your head into a windshield when colliding with another vehicle at sixty-five miles per hour.

Fixx didn't die from smoke inhalation or a car accident, so perhaps he used vehicle seat belts and home smoke detectors. If you want to increase your chances for a long, healthy life, make sure your home is properly protected, and buckle up every time you get in a vehicle.

8. Laugh often, particularly at yourself.

The late Russ Fisher, a humorist and author, said, "Humor is indeed the balancing pole that keeps us on the tightrope of life."[2] Although some people are naturally funny, everyone should develop a sense of humor to offset life's more serious moments. The greatest humor of all is laughing at yourself.

"According to his family," Dr. Cooper reported, "Fixx wasn't very happy . . . he generally felt unfulfilled." Fixx wrote: "For nearly ten years . . . I was bored and restless. The work I was doing wasn't what I wanted to do, and I therefore did not do it very well." He doesn't sound like a man who was able to laugh at himself. He sounds like a man with a broken heart, which ultimately proved true when Fixx burned out for the last time on a lonely New England highway.

Several scientific studies have shown that people of faith are less stressed and happier. In fact Dr. Cooper addressed this subject in *Faith-Based Fitness:* "If you expect your beliefs to have a major impact in motivating you to get fit and stay fit, your deepest personal convictions must be solid and relatively unshakable."[3] He also recommends asking this question: "Do I believe my body is good and worthy of being treated as a creation of God?"

How is your enthusiasm for life? Do you need a boost spiritually, mentally, physically, or emotionally? Which of these life-prolonging habits do you need to embrace? When do you plan to take action? How will you make it happen? Remember, Jim Fixx was physically fit, but he wasn't healthy, and death came earlier than expected.

Choose good health and live a longer, happier, and more energetic life. Don't let an unhealthy lifestyle rob you of your precious time on this earth. Why die before your time? Why not burn as brightly as you can for as long as you can?

13

HARD WORK VS. GOOD HABITS

Hard work, the physical effort necessary for success, is of no value when directed toward the wrong endeavor. You can work hard reshuffling papers already processed, but it's not a productive labor. It's the difference between activity and achievement.

Good habits enable you to work smarter. A discerning carpenter measures twice before cutting once, or a sharp mechanic test-drives your car before tearing it apart. Discipline, the ability to change bad habits into good habits, ensures that hard work is directed toward worthwhile achievement.

Linda Miles, a good friend and one of my mentors, understands why good habits should precede hard work. In 1976 Linda was hired as a dental assistant to Dr. Dick Wilson in Richmond. He encouraged Linda to attend seminars and broaden her dental knowledge. She loved learning and started creating systems to improve office scheduling. Dr. Wilson told his peers about Linda, and other dentists began calling her.

Linda did training sessions on her days off, and her sideline soon became a part-time job. By 1980 she had launched her own dental training business. Today, Linda Miles is a household name in the

dental profession. She has worked hard to earn an impeccable reputation as a keynote speaker, seminar leader, consultant, and author.
If anything, Linda has worked too hard.

At one point Linda was doing eighteen seminars a month and consulting with dentists the rest of the time. Her travel schedule was hectic.
She had ten employees and a huge payroll. She had a 3,500-square-foot
office. Her key staff person was working eighty-hour weeks. Finally, in
1998, Linda ruptured a disk and had back surgery. It was a wake-up call
to work smarter, not harder.

Now Linda does no more than seventy engagements per year. She
no longer consults. She has created the Speaker Consultant Network,
a train-the-trainer program that licenses other speakers to deliver her
programs. She has sold her SunFun cruise seminar business to another
dental enterprise. She has one staff person and a handful of inde-
pendent contractors. She has a 450-square-foot office used primarily
for product storage, but Linda works out of her home. With the
reduced overhead and workload, she's netting the same income, working fewer hours, and feeling much better.

"I've come full circle," said Linda. "The good scheduling habits I
developed for Dr. Wilson enabled me to help other dentists work
smarter. When I went out on my own, I didn't follow my own advice.
I let hard work get the best of me. I had to rethink my business after
back surgery. I'm working smarter. Our product sales remain brisk.
I have a new curriculum for the trainees licensed to use my material, and it's going nationwide. I'm more excited than ever about my
business."

The message is crystal clear. Working smarter is about good habits
and self-discipline. It doesn't mean you shouldn't work hard, but you

shouldn't work all the time. As Dr. Ken Boa says, "There should be a rhythm between work and leisure in our lives so that we can enjoy periods of refreshment, renewal, restoration and relationships. Most of us have a tendency to overvalue work. Work hard, but do not overwork."[1]

The Common Denominator of Success is a classic piece on how to develop good work habits.[2] It was delivered as a speech in 1940 by Albert E. N. Gray, a Prudential insurance executive who addressed the annual convention of the National Association of Life Underwriters in Philadelphia. It was given to me as a pamphlet in 1975. I've read it many times over the years. Here are four of Mr. Gray's greatest thoughts on developing good habits:

1. "The common denominator of success—the secret of success of every person who has ever been successful—lies in the fact that they formed the habit of doing things that failures don't like to do."

   There's no difference between what people who fail don't like to do and what people who are successful don't like to do. Successful people just discipline themselves to do what they don't like to do so they can get what they really want.

   For example, successful life insurance agents dislike rejection as much as unsuccessful agents do. However, top producers work smarter. They know rejection comes with the territory. They do a better job of prospect qualification, which raises closing ratios and lowers frustration levels. They persist until they get what they really want by helping their policyholders get what they want.

2. "Every single qualification for success is acquired through habits. People form habits and habits form futures. If you do not deliberately form good habits, then unconsciously you will form bad ones."

Your habits will make or break you. If you don't form the conscious good habit of setting your alarm clock before going to bed, the unconscious bad habit is possibly oversleeping and missing an important appointment or opportunity.

If a person wants to fail in the life insurance business, he or she will unconsciously form the bad habit of "calling on people who are willing to listen but unable to buy." Successful agents deliberately form the good habit of "calling on people who are able to buy but unwilling to listen." An anonymous writer reminds us of the consequences of our habits:

> Take me, train me, be firm with me
> And I will place the world at your feet.
> Be easy with me and I will destroy you.
> Who am I? I am habit.

3. "Successful people are influenced by the desire for pleasing results. Failures are influenced by the desire for pleasing methods and are inclined to be satisfied with such results as can be obtained by doing things they like to do."

It takes a high degree of self-discipline to be more focused on the big picture than the obstacles along the way. Successful people do what needs to be done to get the results they really want. Failures focus on what they want to do, but rarely end up with what they really need.

Top agents know life insurance isn't about death; it's about providing money for others to go on living when a loved one dies. The pleasant result is an insurance policy that provides such an income. Unsuccessful agents like the pleasant task of figuring out how many policies they'd like to sell. They dislike the unpleasant task of learning about the different insurance products so they can do a better job of educating their prospects.

4. "You will never succeed beyond the purpose to which you are willing to surrender."

What you do isn't as important as *why* you do what you do. If your goals aren't linked to a worthwhile purpose, you'll be doing what's best for you (rights) without thinking about what's best for others (responsibilities).

When a life insurance agent makes the Million Dollar Round Table, he or she has surrendered to a purpose dedicated to serving the policyholders at the highest level of professionalism. The industry recognition and financial rewards are just the personal goals derived from being on-purpose. Agents who concentrate on personal goals without linking them to a higher professional purpose are more likely to fail in the insurance industry.

No matter how successful you become, you'll never eliminate all of your bad habits. The secret is to have more good ones than bad ones, and self-discipline makes this a worthy goal. An undisciplined life is a rocky road. Too many bad habits can sidetrack your journey. In fact the lack of self-discipline is perhaps the biggest killer of achievement.

On the other hand, a life filled with self-discipline and good habits is a beeline to true success and happiness. Yes, hard work is still a requirement, but your good habits will make sure you're achieving the right things while enjoying the ride. It boils down to this: either you're mastered by your bad habits, or you're the master of your good habits.

Are you working too hard? Would you like to work smarter? Do you have some bad habits that need to be converted into good ones? Are you willing to learn from Linda Miles before bad health gets the best of you?

Don't let hard work become your master and turn you into a workaholic. Instead, develop your good habits through self-discipline and enjoy working smarter. Your mind, body, and soul will be forever grateful.

14

TIME STRATEGIES
VS. TIME TACTICS

Time strategies deal with the areas where you spend your life—work, family, place of worship, exercise, and so on. This topic was addressed as managing dominant interests in Chapter 3. Like any strategy, it's a broader plan for how your life will unfold.

Time tactics deal with how you divide each day among your dominant interests. This topic is referred to commonly as time management. Like any tactic, it provides a more specific method for executing a strategy.

Dr. Michael and Audrey Guido are the most meticulous time managers I know. For forty-five years they've directed the Guido Evangelistic Association on a beautiful three-acre campus in Metter, Georgia. They value time based on this motto: "To live well: you must have a faith fit to live by, a self fit to live with, and a work fit to live for." At the ages of eighty-seven and eighty-one, the Guidos understand why each day counts, and they manage each one accordingly.

A typical day starts at 5:00 A.M. with devotions and breakfast. While Audrey cleans up around their home, Michael walks to the office and prays for each employee before they arrive at the office. After a team devotional, Audrey spends her days managing the thirteen-person staff, and Michael works on a variety of publications and broadcasts. After dinner they read and receive phone calls from people who want to talk about their problems. They waste no time.

"It's a rigorous schedule," Dr. Guido concedes, "but I love it. I'd like to find a successor, but it's hard to find someone this dedicated. Sometimes I think the reason we had no children was that the Lord wanted us to be free for the work we're doing." And what a good work they've done through sound time management and an unwavering faith in God.

The Guidos produce three daily radio broadcasts and a daily one-minute telecast. They publish a monthly devotional, newsletter, and sermon. Michael's weekly column is published in more than twelve hundred newspapers. He's a popular guest minister at churches across Georgia—a quiet Billy Graham, I call him. They coauthored *Seeds from the Sower*, a book about their lives and ministry. "Home of the Sower" is the inscription painted on the town water tower in reference to Michael's popular moniker. The I-16 exit to Metter is named the Michael Guido Bridge.

Perhaps more amazing than their time management skills is the Guidos' total trust in God to provide for their ministry. They've never had any debt. They don't sell anything. They send out free information to thirty thousand people each month. They've never asked for donations. When they receive gifts, they always send enthusiastic letters of appreciation. Whenever they have a need, they cut out pictures of these items and pin them on their prayer board. "It's great fun to take the item down a week or month later because the petition has been granted," says Dr. Guido with a big grin.

Indeed, Michael and Audrey get the most out of their treasures, talents, and time—day after day, week after week, year after year. They lead by example. "Preaching without practicing is powerless," Michael warns. You can reach the Guidos at 912-685-2222 or check their Web site at *www.GuidoGardens.org.*

How are you spending each day? Are you organized in such a way to maximize this remarkable resource called time? Just like the Guidos, you have twenty-four hours in each day. Decide which dominant interests are worthy of your attention each day, then create a time slot on your calendar for every prioritized goal within these areas.

Here are Ten Terrific Time-Saving Tactics to help you get more out of each day:

1. Be more focused by using The Master Plan Funnel Concept.

See Chapter 7.

2. Observe the Eight Elite Enhancers of Longer Life.

See Chapter 12.

3. Minimize procrastination by being more decisive.

See Chapter 11.

4. Beware of perfectionism.

Procrastination is never starting, but perfectionism is never finishing.
How do you stand on the following?

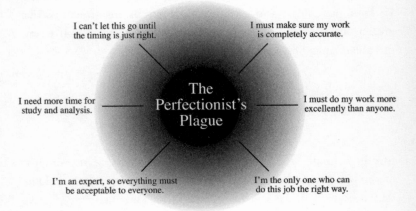

I can't let this go until the timing is just right.

I must make sure my work is completely accurate.

The Perfectionist's Plague

I need more time for study and analysis.

I must do my work more excellently than anyone.

I'm an expert, so everything must be acceptable to everyone.

I'm the only one who can do this job the right way.

5. Learn to say no without feeling guilty.

This is the ultimate time-saver. It doesn't mean you are to avoid serving others. However, it's your life, and you must decide on the wisest use of your time. Don't feel that you have to explain the details of why you can't do something—with the possible exception of your boss. If you say no politely but firmly, that's good enough. Most people will understand your respect for time.

6. Believe that it's easier
to be organized than disorganized.

If you're organized, you know what I mean. If you're not, ask yourself these two questions: *How much time do I waste being disorganized? Once organized, how much more would I get done?* It may take a few weeks to put things in order, but your return on investment will be greater productivity and less stress. An organized life says you're serious about time, life, and others.

7. Eliminate costly time-wasters
such as needless meetings, excessive interruptions,
and unnecessary paperwork.

Meetings should have a specific purpose and agenda. Start promptly, or you penalize the people who are on time. Don't read what could be sent by e-mail or fax. Make meetings fun and interactive. Leave people feeling better than when they arrived. End on time.

Unexpected visits, telephone calls, and e-mail can interrupt your day. You don't have to be rude or unresponsive to people, but learn to be brief or ask if another time would be more convenient. If you don't prioritize your day, it will be prioritized for you. Your productivity will go down, and your frustration level will go up.

Computers have made things more manageable, but they can create a lot more paperwork if you're not careful. Excessive documents create clutter, confusion, and tension. Be a selective reader. Get rid of as much paperwork as possible by acting on it now. Quit e-mailing people endless attachments that aren't absolutely necessary.

8. Use professional advisers and technology.

Are you doing something that someone else could do better? Delegating tasks to others often saves money, and it definitely saves time by allowing you to do what you do best. Do you have the technology to do things more efficiently? Take advantage of these tools, but don't become so addicted to them that you lose the personal touch.

9. Make promptness a good habit.

Regardless of the appointment, be determined to arrive on time. Otherwise, it's easy to fall into the trap of arriving promptly for certain engagements and late for others.

Think through the details of each day's schedule the previous evening. Planning now can save you embarrassment and disappointment later.

Always anticipate unexpected delays by allowing extra time to get where you're going. You can always use any spare minutes wisely if you arrive early, but it's impossible to reclaim lost time, and being late marks you as unreliable.

10. Become an exceptional listener.

The tendency is to hear but not listen to what's being said. Sometimes my wife will ask, "Dick, what did I just say?" If I can't tell her, Judy knows I haven't been listening, and I look foolish. Not only does she have to repeat herself, but it also gives me less time to tell her what I want to say. I've become a better listener because of Judy's "spot checks."

If you really care about a person, you'll pay close attention to the message. Repeat the key points from time to time. Ask questions. Take notes if appropriate. Listen well the first time, and others will be more attentive to your concerns.

The next time you find yourself wasting time, think about a typical day in the lives of Michael and Audrey Guido, the disciplined octogenarians in southeast Georgia. Do you need to reevaluate your time strategies? In which of these ten time tactics are you weakest? What will you do to turn these liabilities into assets?

Franklin Field said, "The great dividing line between success and failure can be expressed in five words: 'I did not have time.'" Your life is a reflection of your time strategies and tactics. What you *do* with each day determines what you'll *become* over your lifetime. Make the time to make it a great life!

15

DESISTING VS. PERSISTING

Desisting means quitting. For example, a cease and desist demand is "an order from an administrative agency to refrain from a method of competition or a labor practice found by the agency to be unfair." Have you ever been treated unfairly and wanted to quit? Do you know people with cease and desist attitudes?

Persisting means going after what you want even when the results aren't going as planned. It's a lifetime commitment achieved through daily devotion to duty. Your life's turning points can be wonderful teachers of persistence.

Martha Berry was born in 1866, the daughter of Captain Thomas Berry, a Civil War veteran and wealthy cotton broker, and Frances Rhea Berry. One Sunday afternoon at an old log cabin near her home at Oak Hill in Rome, Georgia, Martha looked up to see three dirty boys looking in the window. She learned they were from nearby Lavender Mountain, where there was no church or school. Martha told these boys Bible stories, and they returned the next Sunday with more children. What started as a Sunday school class became a boarding school in 1902.

The poor, uneducated mountain kids were eager to hear Miss Berry teach the Bible and other topics of interest. But as more children arrived from across the South, operating costs far exceeded the available funds. Martha wondered how she could keep the school afloat without going bankrupt. She had written many letters asking for donations, but the deficit continued to mount. It would have been easy to desist.

Then, one night in the dormitory, she heard a boy's urgent, sincere prayer at the evening assembly: "I'm wonderin', Lord, whether You ain't showin' the way right now. I read in the paper about some New York people givin' money to schools. Dear God, give Miss Berry strength to get up there and tell them folks how much we need things. Amen."[1] It was a turning point for Martha Berry and her beloved school because she rode the train the following week to New York City.

Martha called on a friend, who arranged for her to speak at a Presbyterian church in Brooklyn. Unable to afford a cab, she took a streetcar through heavy snow and arrived just as the service was ending. The sympathetic minister asked Miss Berry if she would like to say a few words. When she finished telling her stories of the mountain boys, several people offered to provide money and other needs. One couple handed Martha the name of a wealthy Wall Street gentleman: R. Fulton Cutting.

The next day Martha visited Mr. Cutting. He donated $500, enough money to provide scholarships to ten boys. In all she raised $1,700, which was enough to keep the school going through the summer. She also caught pneumonia, and her recovery was in doubt for several days. But when Martha Berry returned to Georgia, she knew that the little boy's prayer had been answered and that the rest of America had begun to hear her story.

Brimming with renewed confidence, Miss Berry crisscrossed the nation over the next few years to talk with numerous influential people. Once, while steel magnate Andrew Carnegie was visiting Atlanta, Martha missed the chance to talk with him due to the crowds. Ever persistent, she boarded Mr. Carnegie's train and had breakfast with him the next morning. This eventually led to another meeting and a $25,000 donation toward a $100,000 endowment—provided she could raise the additional $75,000.

Dr. Albert Shaw, a famous magazine editor, arranged for Martha to tell her story to President Theodore Roosevelt. Moved by her work, President Roosevelt encouraged Martha to add a girls' school, and that became a reality on Thanksgiving Day, 1909. After leaving the White House, President Roosevelt made good on his promise to visit the little Georgia school, which he did on October 8, 1910. Roosevelt called the school "one of the greatest works for American citizenship that has been done within the decade." The building in which he dined became the Roosevelt Cabin.

Over the years, other famous people helped the persistent Martha Berry—Henry Ford, Thomas Edison, Charles Dana, Ida Tarbell, William Jennings Bryan, President Franklin D. Roosevelt, and Eleanor Roosevelt were among them. Martha Berry never married, devoting her life to the education of the boys and girls of the mountains. She died on February 26, 1942, and her portrait now hangs in Georgia's capitol. And it all began with a simple turning point one Sunday afternoon when three mountain boys paid a visit to that log cabin.

Today, this memorial greets visitors at the main entrance of Martha's school in northwest Georgia:

Berry College
Founded By
Martha Berry
1866–1942

Starting with a Sunday school in a log cabin one mile south of here, Martha Berry founded a boarding school for rural boys in 1902 on 83 acres of land, adding a school for girls in 1909. From this humble beginning, Berry College grew and, during Miss Berry's lifetime, became a private educational domain occupying 27,000 acres. Emphasizing high academic standards, Christian values and practical work experience, Berry College is coeducational and offers a wide range of programs to students from all parts of the U.S. and many other countries.

No matter how they begin or end, turning points can offer perspective, which is the ability to view major changes within the larger framework of your lifetime and let the healing power of time prevail. By learning from these significant changes, you can grow and mature at a deeper level within your career and life. And that's what persistence is all about—time, growth, and maturity.

Expect to experience three to nine turning points in your life. These changes can be happy experiences, such as graduating from college, being promoted at work, getting married, having children, and starting a business, or unhappy times, such as losing a job, going through a divorce, experiencing a financial setback or health problems, and losing loved ones through death.

In the following exercise, review your life by listing the years of your turning points, what the changes were, and if enough time has elapsed, what the long-term impact has been:

	YEAR	TURNING POINT	IMPACT
1.	_____	_____	_____
2.	_____	_____	_____
3.	_____	_____	_____
4.	_____	_____	_____
5.	_____	_____	_____
6.	_____	_____	_____
7.	_____	_____	_____
8.	_____	_____	_____
9.	_____	_____	_____

I've asked thousands of people to do this turning point exercise. The following note is typical of the feedback over the years:

I was devastated when my husband died in an automobile accident after 35 years of marriage. I couldn't see how this tragedy could turn into something positive. But five years later, I own a business and I'm doing what I always wanted to do. I loved my husband dearly and think about him every day, but he was old-fashioned and would have discouraged entrepreneurship. Business ownership has helped me deal with my grief. It has opened up opportunities that make every day exciting and fulfilling. I have a new perspective on life. Thank you for encouraging me to examine my turning points.

I can identify with this woman. Seven years after I started my business, the cash flow wasn't flowing. My $50,000 business line of credit was at its limit. I'd delved into all my savings except for some long-term investments. I was considering a second mortgage on our home. If I didn't get some business in the next month, I'd probably have to close down. It was another turning point in my life when desisting looked more likely than persisting.

The next day I received a call from a friend referring me to a company in need of an outside trainer. This prospective client wanted to send two people to audit one of my local seminars. I was elated. Typically twenty people attended these sessions. The day before my big opportunity, I received two cancellation calls within minutes, and my class was cut in half. Nevertheless, I vowed to impress my prospective client with a class of ten people.

The next day I had more no-shows than usual. I was left with one paying attendee at $95 and two guests auditing my seminar at no fee. Who is going to be impressed with a "crowd" of three people at a seminar? Would this seal the fate of my faltering business? Just before the eight o'clock start, one of the guest managers said, "Dick, I know this half-day seminar ends at noon, but we're going to have to leave at the first break."

Life deals some strange hands, but I was in a real bind. I lost money for the day. I was about to go out of business. And in ninety minutes, I was going to be doing a seminar for one person, and there was going to be no energy in the room. In spite of the dire situation, I came out punching and gained the interest of the two visiting managers.

At the first break, they said, "Dick, we're staying for the rest of the seminar and taking you to lunch." Our meal lasted three hours. They hired me as an outside trainer for a project that lasted more than a year and turned my business around. Years later, I'm still feeling the positive impact of this turning point.

Are you experiencing a challenge that has you ready to desist? Will you do the turning point exercise and look for positives from these transitional times? Will you keep on keeping on, never underestimating the awesome power of persistence? Like Martha Berry, will you allow special people to help you through difficult times? Is there a "three-person seminar" about to unfold in your life and teach you a valuable lesson?

Don't let your turning points get you too up or too down. These significant changes can offer valuable perspective found rarely in the mundane moments of life. If you desist, you'll never know what could have been. When you persist, you open up a world of opportunities that make every day exciting and fulfilling. You'll persist, won't you?

16

MASTERED BY CHANGE VS. MASTERING CHANGE

Are you mastered by change? Are you in a rut and still digging? Do you find yourself saying things like these: "We've always done it this way . . . I dread learning a new system . . . I wish these changes would just go away"?

Or are you a change master? Do you get excited about new ways to do old things? Do you welcome opportunities to learn and grow by getting out of your comfort zone? Are you willing to take risks even when you're ridiculed and second-guessed?

Dr. Ignaz Philipp Semmelweis was a legendary change master. He stepped out of his comfort zone, took a huge risk, and in the mid-1800s changed the medical field forever. Born in 1818, this Hungarian gynecologist had an impact on medical history that is felt every day in hospitals around the world. We owe a big debt of gratitude to a man who had the courage of his convictions, a hero willing to implement a new and better idea.

It's hard to believe now, but one out of eight mothers died from childbirth fever in the mid-nineteenth century. While serving at the renowned Vienna General Hospital in Austria, Dr. Semmelweis observed physicians performing autopsies, then examining expectant mothers without washing their hands. In fact Dr. Jakob Kolletschka, his closest friend, died shortly after cutting his finger while performing an autopsy.

Dr. Semmelweis was the first to associate such examinations with infection and death. He used a chlorine solution and lost 1 mother in 50 after delivering 8,537 babies in 11 years. His findings were published in *The Etiology, Concept and Prophylaxis of Childbirth Fever,* but most doctors ignored the book.

His peers ridiculed Dr. Semmelweis, who refused to give up on a procedure he knew was right. He spent hours lecturing on his simple procedure and debating with his colleagues. He pleaded with them to change but was met with fierce resistance. He wrote in frustration: "Puerperal [childbirth] fever is caused by decomposed material conveyed to a wound. I have shown how it can be prevented. I have proven all that I have said. But while we talk, talk, talk, gentlemen, women are dying. I am not asking anything world-shaking. I am only asking that you wash . . . for God's sake, wash your hands!"

Dr. Semmelweis spent the best years of his short life trying to convince the medical profession to change. His crusade led to mental illness, insanity, and death at the age of forty-seven. His associates were probably laughing in his face while thousands of pregnant women died because doctors were too proud to wash their hands.

In 1865, the year of Semmelweis's death, Dr. Joseph Lister performed his first antiseptic operation. It was soon acknowledged that Semmelweis had been right. This brave change master is known as "the Father of Infection Control." He is honored by an Edouard Chassaing sculpture standing in the Hall of Medical Immortals in Chicago.

Doing your best often means changing even when it's unpopular. Dr. Semmelweis died trying to get others to change, but millions of people have lived because of this man's determination. When you become a change master, you open up a world of endless possibilities. Of course, there are truths that never change, so you need the wisdom to know what to alter and what to leave alone.

Here are four unique perspectives on dealing successfully with the challenge of change:

1. No Change Is Impossible

We lived at ten addresses in five cities by my seventeenth birthday. I attended three elementary schools, two high schools, and three colleges. In my four years of active duty in the Marines, I was stationed in nine places. I've had three careers—a short one in journalism, thirteen years in sales, and twenty as a business owner. As a professional speaker, I have to change constantly to meet the specific needs of each client.

If you've experienced a lot less change, look at the world around you. In the past century, there has been more change than all the other centuries combined. Here's an A to Z summary: airplanes, bionics, cars, deregulation, electronic mail, fax machines, genetics, hydrogen bombs, Internet, junk bonds, karate, lasers, MRIs, nuclear power, overnight delivery, pagers, quantum theory, radios, satellites, televisions, ultrasound, VCRs, the wellness movement, Xerox machines, yellow pages, and zippers. It's just a partial list, with most of these changes coming in the last half of the twentieth century.

2. Some Change Is Impractical

"Changing Times, Unchanging Truths" is an article available on my Web site at biggspeaks.com. It's an interview with George Washington as if he were alive today. The first American president is delighted with the economic and technological changes that have occurred since he went out of office more than two hundred years ago, but he is appalled by the moral decay of modern America.

Washington states in the mock interview: "America was founded on Judeo-Christian principles. Since these principles were good enough to establish our nation, I believe they're good enough to help us endure as a nation." In short, the truths of the Bible, God's Holy Word, have remained changeless for centuries. People can rationalize their immoral behavior because "everybody else is doing it," but it doesn't make these truths any less applicable.

3. Most Change Is Uncomfortable

Making any change can be a headache, but not changing can cause heartache. Turning points are often very uncomfortable times and can become headaches. But if you don't change, the resulting heartache can be more painful. Without that referral and three-person seminar discussed in Chapter 15, I probably wouldn't be in business today.

When you face uncomfortable changes and painful turning points, Tom Hopkins offers this sage advice: "The pain of every change is forgotten when the benefits of that change are realized."[1] If you're a mother, you have a firsthand understanding of this truth because childbirth is no picnic. If you're a working man, you know your career wouldn't be where it is today without some growing pains along the way. The joy of any success is almost always preceded by the agony of some mistakes, disappointments, and pain.

4. Every Change Has Consequences

When the postal service raises rates, customers experience an economic jolt. Whether the stock market rises or falls, investors feel the impact. When laws are enacted to crack down on certain crimes, convicted violators suffer the consequences of punishment. When politicians fail to serve their constituents, they risk becoming ex-politicians the next time voters go to the polls. When major corporations merge, some employees often lose their jobs or take early retirement.

The question isn't, "Will change bring consequences?" The question is, "Will the consequences of this change make me better off in the long run than I am today?" If you resist change, you'll continue to get what you've always gotten. If you embrace change, you have the opportunity to enjoy bountiful benefits reserved only for people willing to take risks and get out of their comfort zones.

What changes are holding you back from reaching your full potential? Do you need to take more risks? Do you need to step outside your comfort zone and dare to be better than you are? Like Dr. Semmelweis, will you be a change master no matter what others might say? Will you endure some short-term pain for much long-term gain? Or are you waiting until the pain of not changing becomes greater than the pain of changing?

Have the courage of your convictions. Give yourself a chance for good things to happen. Be like Simon Peter who, after fishing all night with his friends and catching nothing, stepped out in faith and obeyed this commandment by Jesus: "Now go out where it is deeper and let down your nets, and you will catch many fish" (Luke 5:4). The story tells us, "Both boats were filled with fish and on the verge of sinking" (v. 7), because the men had the fortitude to leave shallow waters and launch out into the deep.

17

STRESS VS. SERENITY

Stress is your body's reaction to change, challenge, coercion, or lack of control. It alters your equilibrium and can cause anxiety, depression, exhaustion, illness, or even death. The Latin derivation means to be "drawn tight" or, in modern terms, to be "uptight."

Serenity is a state of peacefulness designed to relieve your tension. Frankly a stress-free life would be boring. On the other hand, a stressed-out life can lead to burnout—and worse. Somewhere between boring and burnout is a balance based on managing stress by making time for serenity.

Years ago, while participating in a planning retreat for the Georgia Speakers Association (GSA), I learned an important lesson about balancing stress with serenity. Our committee had spent the previous day and most of the morning revising the GSA purpose statement, deciding on annual goals, and developing action plans. The tedious work left us tired and stressed out.

Sensing our mental and physical fatigue, the session facilitator said, "Instead of taking the usual ten-minute break to rush to the telephone, here's what I'd like you to do. Take a thirty-minute break, but spend the time alone on this lovely property. Try not to think about GSA or your business. Just find a quiet spot and relax. Go now."

I headed for a trail that led to a river on the perimeter of the resort. It was a humid July day in the north Georgia mountains, but the heavy forest offered shade and the water provided a refreshing mist. About ten minutes into my tranquillity, I heard voices and observed three men coming down to the trail. A middle-aged man and two younger fellows were dressed in hard hats, sweaty T-shirts, shorts, and work boots. They stripped down to their shorts and waded into the river to cool off.

When they emerged from the water, I asked the men what brought them to this resort. The oldest man replied, "We're working on a roof up here while waiting for another big job in Atlanta. We usually build skyscrapers, so this is like a vacation."

"Skyscrapers!" I exclaimed. "That's pretty stressful work, isn't it?"

The veteran worker responded, "Well, you sort of get used to it. You just walk around all day on narrow beams and weld them together. Nothing to it."

"Yeah," I answered, "but one slip and it's all over. Aren't you afraid to be up that high?"

"Sir," said the construction man, "if you don't mind my asking, what do you do for a living?"

"I'm a professional speaker."

"Now that's what I call a scary job," said the steelworker, with fear in his eyes. "I once gave a ten-minute talk at AA. Man, I was a nervous wreck. My knees were wobbling, and my teeth were chattering. I was sweating from head to foot. I could never speak for a living. It's way too stressful."

"Are you telling me you'd rather work thirty floors up than speak to a group of thirty people?"

"That's right, but you have to understand something. I've been working on tall buildings most of my life. To me, it's not all that stressful. Fortunately each building starts on the ground floor, and we work our way up one story at a time. You get used to the height. You learn to concentrate on what you're doing and not think about falling. I'm sure your first speech was nerve-wracking, but you had to start somewhere, right?"

"Absolutely. My first audience was about twenty people, and I was stressed out. I figured if I messed up, it would be a learning experience, and only a few people would know about my folly. I suppose it's similar to starting out on the ground floor of a skyscraper. If you mess up, it's not fatal, but your confidence grows and you keep on going, right?"

The steelworker nodded in agreement. "You know, I guess the mark of any pro is that he or she makes a difficult job look easy. What's stressful to one person is enjoyable to another. But as much as I love my work, I need time away from the job. I bet you feel the same way about speaking. It's obvious you love what you do, but anything done to excess can become stressful. I'm sure you enjoy some time away from your audiences, don't you?"

"More than you know," I replied. "In fact, I'm up here with some of my peers working on the coming year for our professional association. We've been working hard since yesterday morning, and we're all stressed out. Our facilitator gave us thirty minutes of quiet time, and it's the reason I'm here talking to you."

"Well, it hasn't been a very quiet time for you, has it?"

"Actually," I responded, "you've taught me a valuable lesson about balancing stress with serenity. Life is no different from building a skyscraper or delivering a speech. When you master your life's work, you minimize stress and make what you do look effortless to others. But if you don't make time for serenity, it's easy to become a stressed-out workaholic."

We shook hands, and the three men headed up the trail. I enjoyed my last few minutes of serenity by the riverbank before returning to the more stressful meeting.

To burn brightly without burning out, you should offset the stresses of society with times of tranquillity in the spiritual, mental, physical, and emotional sides of your life. Here are some stress relievers in these four areas:

Spiritual

I try to make time for a daily devotional—Bible reading, prayer, and quiet time with God. I'm active in my church, where Judy and I lead a small group in Bible study. Prior to that, I taught Sunday school for fifteen years. I work on teams for the Walk to Emmaus, a nondenominational Christian retreat that takes place over a three-day period at locations around the world. I read Christian books.

Depending upon your worldview, spiritual stress relief might be taking a walk in nature. It might be participating in a community project or going on a mission trip. It might be serving in a soup kitchen. It might mean belonging to a civic or garden club. What's important is that when you help others and turn to God, you tend to forget about your own troubles while gaining necessary stress relief and divine guidance.

Mental

I work crossword puzzles every day for a few minutes. When I started years ago, it was very stressful because I couldn't finish a single one. Now, I love the mental relaxation of finishing what I start. I also love playing Scrabble. I go to a quiet park about once a month to read and reflect.

Are you making time to stimulate your mind away from the office and the daily grind? Do you have a program for your personal growth? Are you so stressed out by work that you have no time to think about anything else? I urge you to find an enjoyable mental outlet. Your inner peace will soar, and your cerebral stress will sag.

Physical

Exercise is a terrific stress reliever. I prefer running, but I also walk periodically. There are many beautiful trails surrounding Lake Lanier, my home just north of Atlanta. It makes exercising more than a physical workout—it's also a spiritual, mental, and emotional revitalization. When traveling, I look for tranquil spots to exercise—historic battlefields, ocean settings, peaceful parks, or river trails. A change of scenery keeps exercise fun and exciting.

If you dislike running, try hiking, biking, swimming, or rowing. Participate in a team sport like volleyball, basketball, or softball. Play tennis or golf. Work vigorously in the yard or garden, but do something physical for needed stress relief. As Nolan Ryan, baseball's all-time strikeout leader, says, "If you can't control your body, you can't control your mind. Make an appointment with yourself to exercise and keep it."

Emotional

I like to have things to look forward to that offset the emotional stress of society. My feelings get frazzled with the demands of everyday life. Judy and I plan our tranquil times for the coming year during the week between Christmas and New Year. We schedule long weekend getaways, retreats, and vacations. We've found if we don't plan some of our serenity, the year has a way of getting away from us, and we get stressed out.

The anticipation of these events is a stress reliever in itself.

What are you doing for emotional stress relief? Most of life's turmoil is out of your control, but you can take charge of your serenity. You owe it to yourself, your family, and your friends to offset the emotional eruptions of this world with some tranquil times. Enjoy them. Make the most of them. Cherish them. Your mind, body, and spirit will be healthier and happier.

Are you stressed out? Are you burned out? Are you out of balance spiritually, mentally, physically, and emotionally? Do you long for more serenity but just can't seem to make it happen? How are you doing with these "Top Ten Stressors" from a magazine survey?[1]

1. Personal finances

2. Career

3. Too many responsibilities

4. Marriage

5. Health

6. Children

7. Loneliness

8. Sex

9. Relatives

10. Neighbors

The skyscraper workman was right. You can't live a balanced life when you're stressed out. It's also utopian to seek a stress-free life. Manage your external pressures (stress) by making time for internal peace (serenity), and watch your quality of life go from punishing to rewarding.

18

URGENT VS. IMPORTANT

Urgent is now. While also important, urgent matters demand immediate attention due to the pressing nature of the situation. If you're about to have a head-on vehicle collision, it's urgent to take evasive action at once, or you and others could suffer serious injury or death.

Important is over a lifetime. Urgency sets in only when you fail to accomplish your goals late in life. If writing a book is important and you're ninety years old, it's also urgent because you're beyond the average life expectancy.

Urgent and important matters are concerned with time—one short term, the other long term. The Greeks thought so much of time they had two words for it—*chronos* and *kairos*. *Chronos* is the root of *chronology,* which deals with the measurement of time. It's the urgent ticking of the clock and turning of the calendar. *Kairos* means special time. It's when you must make an important decision—a time in which you're caught up in the moment and everything hinges upon whether you say "yes" or "no."

Chronos and *kairos* are contrasted vividly by a wedding. The bride and groom arrive at the church and go to their separate rooms to primp. There's a sense of urgency. And while the big moment is near, the couple remains in *chronos*. They still can change their minds.

The processional begins. The sense of urgency is heightened. The bride, poised and beautiful, walks toward the altar and wonders, *How long will it take to change his bad habits?* The groom, wheezing and perspiring, admires his fiancée and thinks, *Life, as I've known it, is never going to be the same again.* Even at this late hour, they're still in *chronos*. They could refuse to go through with the ceremony.

The bride and groom join the pastor. Hearts are pounding with a solemn sense of urgency. Songs are played. Scripture is read. A prayer is offered. A short message is delivered. And although it would be an embarrassing, expensive decision, the man and woman could refuse to say the vows. They're still in *chronos*.

Finally the pastor says, "Do you, Mary, take Steve to be your lawful wedded husband . . ." and, baby, it's *kairos*—special time, an important time in which you're caught up in the moment and everything hinges upon whether you say "yes" or "no."

Do you struggle with what you need to do now (urgent) and what you want to do over a lifetime (important)? If so, welcome to the world of trying to balance the work you need with the life you lead. The following exercise may help you appreciate any imbalance you may be experiencing between the urgent and important matters of your life. In the left column, write down all your urgencies from the past week. In the right column, list what's important during your lifetime:

URGENT *(NOW)*	IMPORTANT *(LIFETIME)*
_____	_____
_____	_____
_____	_____
_____	_____
_____	_____
_____	_____
_____	_____
_____	_____

If it was difficult to fit all your urgencies from the past week in such a small space, that's understandable. A typical week is filled with a myriad of activities requiring immediate attention. There's the pressure of driving to work in rush-hour traffic. There's the stress of flying from city to city. There's the tension of getting to your kid's sporting event or school play. There are deadlines at work. If you kept track of your urgencies for a year, you would have a long, overwhelming list.

Now, take time to think about the important matters of your lifetime. The small space on the right side should provide ample room. I'm not kidding. Do you remember when Air Force Captain Scott O'Grady was shot down over Bosnia? Enemy troops hunted him for a week before a Marine rescue unit intervened. In his account of that tense week, Captain O'Grady explains, "I realized that only three things mattered in this world . . . faith in God . . . the love of family and friends . . . [and] good health."[1]

Like Captain O'Grady's list, the important matters of my life fit in the small space on the right-hand side. I summarized them in Chapter 2 as my purpose statement:

1. I will strive "to do what is right" by maintaining integrity in all facets of daily living.

2. I will strive "to love mercy" by having a positive influence on others as a principle-centered role model and mentor.

3. I will strive "to walk humbly with . . . God" through congruency between my beliefs and behavior.

Part 1 includes being true to myself in business, financial matters, and health/leisure. Part 2 includes relationships with my family, friends, and community. Part 3 includes honoring God with my words and ways.

If you're struggling with what's important in your life, the following questions may be a helpful accountability exercise:

• When you were younger, do you recall the things you wanted most out of life?

• At this point in your life, what are the most important things you have now?

• If you had only a year to live, would your "most important" list change?

In my younger days, making money was more important than anything. My sense of urgency was poor. As I've matured into my fifties, making a difference in the lives of others has become more important than making money (more on this in Chapter 20). My sense of urgency is keener. If I had only one year to live, I'd want more intimacy with God. I suspect my sense of urgency would be even sharper.

The harsh reality is that life is a constant shuffling of the urgent and important.

It's difficult to plan for the unexpected urgencies of life. How can you anticipate the accidental death of a loved one or a bout with cancer? You can, however, develop a more discerning sense of urgency to free up additional time for the important matters that shape the rest of your life. Otherwise, it's easy to convince yourself that everything is urgent, leaving little or no time for the important moments of a lifetime.

Have "urgent" matters taken control of your life? Do you feel as though the fast track has turned into a treadmill to nowhere? Could you use more *kairos* moments and less *chronos* time? Do you need to take inventory of what's really important in life, just as Captain O'Grady did while experiencing an urgent week in Bosnia?

Don't let the pressing matters of work and everyday living sap your energy for the few significant times that will mark your legacy. In the long run, your faith, family, friends, and fitness will mean more to you than anything gained from free enterprise and financial rewards. Each day is a precious gift from God. Make each one count by placing a higher value on the important than on the urgent.

19

PROFESSIONAL SUCCESS VS. PERSONAL HAPPINESS

Professional success is measured externally for the most part. Tangible possessions such as homes, automobiles, boats, recreational vehicles, clothes, jewelry, country club memberships, stocks, bonds, and savings tend to determine your level of prosperity.

Personal happiness is measured internally at the highest level. Intangibles such as being true to yourself, encouraging others, and serving God are the marks of true fulfillment. While professional success is a part of your personal happiness, no amount of career achievement can atone for failure in your personal life.

Joe Black, a fellow speaker and author, taught me a meaningful life lesson on the difference between professional success and personal happiness. Joe tells a poignant story about the best gift a son can give a father—the gift of time. One night while his father was visiting, Joe asked, "Dad, what place in the United States would you most like to visit that you haven't seen?" His father replied, "The Rocky Mountains of Colorado." On Father's Day week, Joe gave his seventy-three-year-old father an all-expense-paid trip to the vacation spot of his dreams.[1]

As I read Joe's stirring account of this memorable week with his father, I wept. It made me want to take a similar trip. About a month later, my father traveled from Florida to visit us in Georgia. One night after dinner, I asked, "Dad, what place in the United States would you most like to visit that you haven't seen?" He answered without hesitation, "The Grand Canyon." A few weeks later on Father's Day, I called and said, "Dad, I'd like for the two of us to go to the Grand Canyon the week of your seventy-second birthday. The trip's on me. What do you think?"

Labor Day week, 1993, we made that trip. We flew first-class from Atlanta to Phoenix on Sunday. We rented a car and drove north to Carefree, where Dad enjoyed his favorite dessert—ice cream. We stopped in Sedona and took several photographs of the unusual reddish mountains. We proceeded along the circuitous road through Oak Creek Canyon before arriving at our motel in Williams, "The Gateway to the Grand Canyon."

On Monday we toured Flagstaff, Sunset Crater National Monument, and Humphreys Peak—the highest point in Arizona at 12,633 feet. On Tuesday we had breakfast at the Old Smoky Pancake House in Williams before the hour drive to the South Rim of the Grand Canyon. This ancient multicolored vista is 10 miles wide, 1 mile deep, and 280 miles long. As he viewed this panoramic wonder from 7,000 feet in elevation, Dad exclaimed, "We build computers and think we're so smart, but only God could have built this."

We stayed at the El Tovar, an extraordinary hotel built in the early twentieth century on the edge of the South Rim. On Wednesday we took a three-hour bus ride to Glen Canyon Dam at Lake Powell, the start of our raft ride down the aqua waters of the Colorado River. We marveled at the limestone walls rising to 1,500 feet on both sides of Marble Canyon. Our guide gave us the most serene four-hour ride imaginable. By the time we reached Lees Ferry, our concluding point and the start of the Grand Canyon, the river had turned muddy and the first rapids were in sight.

We spent Thursday visiting several scenic overlooks along the South Rim. At Mather Point we noticed a young lady sitting perilously close to the canyon edge. Dad asked her if she was okay. We learned later that three people fell to their deaths that week. Dad wondered if that young lady was one of them. We had dinner that evening at the Arizona Steak House and witnessed a magnificent sunset. Our conversation covered topics we hadn't discussed in years.

On Friday we had an enjoyable drive back to Phoenix, where we spent the evening in the shadows of Camelback Mountain. After dinner we watched the Atlanta Braves finally catch the San Francisco Giants after being down nine and a half games just weeks earlier. We flew back to Atlanta on Saturday. A few days later, I received a thank-you card with these words etched on the outside: "There's a special kind of love the heart reserves just for a son." This handwritten note appeared on the inside: "My heartfelt thanks for the wonderful trip and opportunity for us to be together. It was a once-in-a-lifetime experience. I will always be grateful. I love you . . . Dad."

It would have been easy to rationalize all the reasons I couldn't be away from my work for a week by saying, "I don't want to spend that much money. I don't want to miss any speaking engagements. I don't want to lose an entire week of marketing. I don't want to lose any potential revenue." But in getting away from the stress of business and the opportunity for more professional success, I gained tranquil time with my father and a lot of personal happiness. How do you put a dollar value on a family memory that will last a lifetime?

Happiness has been defined in many ways, but it's often difficult to discover. To find more joy in life, consider the "6 Fs" and "2 Hs" of true happiness:

Faith

What is faith? It is the confident assurance that what we hope for is going to happen. It is the evidence of things we cannot yet see.

—HEBREWS 11:1

Faith in God is a spiritual thing, not a physical thing that can be proven. I choose to have faith in God, even though I've never seen God. Anyone who treats faith in God like a science is missing the very essence of faith. It can't be put under a microscope or demonstrated like the theory of gravity. It's a conviction felt on the inside and capable of moving mountains on the outside. When we don't trust God, there's no hope for a better life. With God, all things are possible.

Freedom

Freedom without limits brings chaos.

—DONALD E. WILDMAN

In America we enjoy abundant blessings because we live in a free society and work in a free enterprise system. Our Constitution guarantees us certain freedoms—of religion, the press, assembly, speech, and others.

Humankind was meant to be free, but freedom isn't free. The price tag is responsibility.

Family

The foundation of civilization and human relationships is the family.

—DR. LAURA C. SCHLESSINGER

The family is the most basic unit of society, and it's more dysfunctional than ever. Parents should give their children a set of moral absolutes, then warn them about the consequences of violating these principles. Parents should hold their children accountable for their actions and encourage them to stand up for their rights without falling down on their responsibilities. Spouses should take their marriage vows seriously, serving as exemplary role models and mentors for their children.

Friends

One friend in a life is much, two are many, three are hardly possible.

—HENRY BROOKS ADAMS

I have hundreds of acquaintances but only a handful of good friends. Good friends share in your successes and setbacks. They provide unconditional love, with no expectations in return. A good friendship requires time based on many shared experiences. Trust and friendship are inseparable. Good friends know when to talk and when to listen. Above all, good friends are forgiving and respectful of each other.

Fraternalism

The unselfish love and concern for the welfare of others.

—WEBSTER'S DICTIONARY

This is your outreach beyond family and friends. It's about serving your community and helping people less fortunate than you. Are you donating food and clothes to a neighborhood charity? Are you assisting people in trouble on the highway? Are you giving blood to the Red Cross? Are you ringing the bell for The Salvation Army at Christmas? Are you mentoring a child at a local school? Are you volunteering at a hospital or nursing home?

Forgiveness

*Only the brave know how to forgive . . . a coward never forgave;
it is not in his [or her] nature.*

—LAURENCE STERNE

You can't be happy if you're always mad at someone about something. Not only is forgiveness biblical, it's necessary to maintain an orderly society. Imagine how chaotic the world would be if revenge were the chief motivator in life. A forgiving spirit doesn't mean a person is weak. On the contrary it takes a strong, courageous person to cast aside his ego and say, "I forgive you." The greatest reward of forgiveness is freedom.

And who knows? In time you might even forget.

Health

The first wealth is health.

—RALPH WALDO EMERSON

Chapter 12 discussed the Eight Elite Enhancers of Longer Life, so I'll add only this: Remember that good health is fragile. Do everything you can to protect it, because it's hard to be happy when you don't feel good.

Hope

There is no medicine like hope, no incentives so great, and no tonics so powerful as expectation of something better tomorrow.

—ORISON SWETT MARDEN

Hope keeps you going. It's the awesome force that propels you into action. It's the wind that breathes in new life when you've been knocked down. It's the sparkle that gives you the courage to try again on another day. As Andy (portrayed by Tim Robbins) said in *The Shawshank Redemption,* a movie about a man who spent twenty years in jail for a crime he didn't commit: "Hope is a good thing."

Has professional success interfered with your personal happiness? Do you need some "Rocky Mountain" and "Grand Canyon" experiences to appreciate the rest of your life? How are you doing with your faith, freedom, family, friends, fraternalism, and forgiveness? How's your health? Are you full of hope?

Channing Pollock, an American playwright and critic, stated, "Happiness is a way-station between too little and too much." Learn the proper balance between professional success and personal happiness, and live life to its fullest.

20

MAKING MONEY VS. MAKING A DIFFERENCE

Making money is necessary to sustain a living. But no matter how much money you earn in a lifetime, these assets become the property of others at your death. In short, your money won't be going with you to the grave.

Making a difference is about your legacy. It's how others will remember you. Unlike money, your legacy can never be taken away, and it goes with you to the grave. As Joseph Addison said in *The Spectator*: "Death only closes a [person's] reputation, and determines it as good or bad."

Eva Bullington Hall, my maternal grandmother, never made much money, but she made a big difference in the lives of the people closest to her. She lived most of her life in Newport, a small town in the Great Smoky Mountains of eastern Tennessee. She had little formal education and was a housewife all her adult life. Grandmother Hall lived through four wars, the Great Depression, the accidental death of her youngest daughter (my aunt Edith), and the agonizingly slow death of Samuel Joseph Hall, her husband of sixty-two years.

At the funeral Grandmother Hall made us promise to visit her as soon as possible.

Six months later, Judy and I returned to Newport. We had originally scheduled our trip for the last weekend in June but changed to the weekend of June 22–23 at the last minute. While still grieving her loss, Grandmother seemed healthy and alert. We tried to take her out to dinner Saturday night, but she insisted on cooking a home-cooked meal. I agreed, provided she'd let us take her into town for an ice-cream cone.

On Sunday morning—June 23, 1985, and exactly two months before Grandmother's eightieth birthday—we enjoyed a delicious country breakfast, then moved to the front porch with the majestic Smoky Mountains in view. I asked Grandmother Hall about the family tree. She talked for three hours, proudly reciting generations on both sides of the family all the way back to the Civil War—names, relationships, dates of death. I took notes and diagrammed the family tree.

Finally she said to me, the oldest of eight grandchildren: "Dick, I haven't been real successful in life. I haven't done a lot of things, gone a lot of places, or had a lot of money. But if I've done nothing else, I've tried to raise my three children the best way I knew how by setting a good example for them and you grandchildren." We left about an hour later. Grandmother Hall waved a tearful farewell.

When we walked into our home late that Sunday evening, the telephone was ringing.

I sensed something was wrong. It was my mother. "Dick," she said slowly, "I have some bad news. Your grandmother died of a massive stroke about an hour after you left. You and Judy were the last ones to see her alive."

When we returned two days later for the funeral, I was thinking about two things. First, I was relieved we'd changed the date of our visit, or I would have missed that memorable time on the front porch and the invaluable family history. More important, I thought: *Grandmother Hall, you were a success more than you'll ever know. You had honesty and integrity, and you modeled these qualities to the people closest to you—your children and grandchildren. You made a difference with your life.*

Making money *is* important, but it's probably not going to be what people think of when they remember you. For example, have you ever seen any of these tombstone inscriptions?

- He was the wealthiest man in town.

- She was a great socialite but didn't have any friends.

- He was too busy to have time for a spiritual life.

- She gave her kids everything but time and love.

Making a difference is more important than making money. You make a difference by passing on your life lessons to others. It's how legitimate legacies are earned. It's the way true success is achieved. Indeed, your legacy is best secured when you help your successors become successful.

The most important legacy you can leave is your intangible spirit, which is passed on by the life you lead. This will have more long-term impact than any tangibles you transfer by will or trust agreement. Of course, there's nothing wrong with great wealth as long as you don't sacrifice your reputation for riches. Money without morality leads to greed. Money with morality fosters generosity.

Earl Masters made a big difference in my life. He was a master salesman and earned a good income most of his life. I lost a memorable friend and mentor on December 6, 1993, but his legacy is clear, as expressed in these words from one of his eulogists:

- He was true to himself [integrity].
- He was an encourager of others [inspiration].
- He was a humble servant of God [influence].
- He lives on after death [immortality].

Your eulogy probably won't be based on how you earned your living; it will be based on the reputation you earned while living. Live with integrity. Be a source of inspiration to others. Let your influence be a reflection of your Creator. Choose eternal life for true immortality.

Is making money your chief motivation in life? Have the demands of business left you empty and unfulfilled? Would you like for life to be more meaningful? Do you long to make a difference the way Grandmother Hall did? Will your legacy be as noble as the one left by Earl Masters?

Never forget that making money is about material success, which dies the minute you do. Will you use money greedily or generously? Always remember that making a difference is about true success, which lives forever in the minds of others. Will your legacy be lowly or legitimate?

EPILOGUE

The great secret in life is learning to do. Decide what you want, learn how to do it and then do it. Do it over and over again until you get the same results that others have.

—BRIAN TRACY

As you've read and reflected on these twenty contrasts of life, have you decided what you'll be doing in the area of work/life balance? Perhaps the following tool will help you take the appropriate action:

The Priority Sieve

This sieve enables you to process the facts (or whats) through a finely screened filter (so what?) before deciding if focused action is required (now what?). You can't do everything, and you certainly can't change things overnight, but you can do something starting right now to have a more balanced lifestyle.

The following headline, which accompanied a *USA Today* cover story, says a lot about our workaholic world: "24/7 almost a way of life . . . more businesses stay open all night to serve a nation that never sleeps."[1] It's indicative of a burned-out society. Cheerful hearts have been exchanged for broken spirits. Service and significance have been bypassed in the furious quest for silver and success. It doesn't have to be that way.

Humankind is unique among all living things. You have the freedom and intelligence to choose your way of life. You can refuse the 24/7 treadmill. Yes, you may have to work fewer hours and even settle for less income. Yes, you may have to reduce your expenses and save more money. And, yes, you may have to leave the rat race for the human pace of a more simplified lifestyle.

Og Mandino knew all about the struggle to burn brightly without burning out. Early in his career, he was a successful life insurance agent. However, his long hours at the office and excessive drinking caused problems at home. His wife and children left him. Og lost his family, home, and job. Nearly penniless, he became a gypsy, working odd jobs and often sleeping in his car. He was devastated, disillusioned, and burned out.

One cold, rainy day in Cleveland, with only thirty dollars in his pocket, Og walked down the street intent on suicide. He stopped in front of a gun shop and eyed a cheap weapon. For some reason, Og walked on until reaching a library. He began to read *Success Through a Positive Mental Attitude* by Napoleon Hill and W. Clement Stone. Og left that Cleveland library a changed man. He vowed to make something of his life and to burn brightly from that moment on.

Og called on W. Clement Stone, the founder and chairman of Combined Insurance Company of America in Chicago. Mr. Stone published a magazine titled *Success Unlimited,* and Og eventually became executive editor. In 1968 Og authored his first book, and it became a phenomenal best-seller. *The Greatest Salesman in the World* has sold millions of copies and has been translated into many languages.

In 1976 Og resigned his position at *Success Unlimited* to become a full-time writer and speaker. He has helped thousands of people with books such as *The Greatest Secret in the World, The Greatest Mystery in the World, The Greatest Miracle in the World, The Greatest Success in the World, The Choice, A Better Way to Live, The Return of the Ragpicker, The Christ Commission, Mission: Success!,* and many others. The first recipient of the Napoleon Hill Gold Medal for literary achievement, Og is one of the greatest inspirational authors of all time.

And yet, if this remarkable influencer had burned out that rainy day in Cleveland, we would have missed out on a wealth of encouragement from a master storyteller and eloquent wordsmith. I met Og twice at National Speakers Association conventions. He was a humble man who cared about his audiences. He was gracious enough to pose for a photograph, and I display it proudly on my office wall.

I also have taped to my computer desk this quote from *The Greatest Mystery in the World*: "When you get into a tight place and everything goes against you, till it seems as though you could not hold on a minute longer, never give up then, for that is just the place and time that the tide will turn." I'm thankful Og was able to hold on and burn brightly for so many years. He passed away in 1996, but his books continue to sell briskly and offer a beacon of hope to people around the world.

What are you hoping for? Are you competing for earthly possessions that will be insignificant when you die? Or are you seeking something more lasting? Both King Solomon and Og Mandino burned out chasing the wind of the secular lifestyle. They learned how to burn brightly after discovering that wisdom comes when you fear God enough to seek His timeless truths instead of the temporary trappings of the world.

Here are the choices you must make: Will you burn brightly with a cheerful heart? Or will you burn out and be left with a broken spirit? Will you balance the work you need with the life you lead? Will you recognize that no amount of professional success can replace the joy of being true to yourself, serving others, and honoring your Creator?

I'm praying you'll make the right decisions. God bless you always.

NOTES

INTRODUCTION

1. *America @ Work: An Overview of Employee Commitment in America, 1998, www.aonconsulting.com*

2. Pamela Kruger, *Fast Company,* February 1997.

3. *Fortune,* 9 July 2001.

4. *The Kiplinger Letter,* 28 June 2002.

5. *USA Today* guest column, 1 October 2001.

CHAPTER 12

1. Dr. Kenneth H. Cooper, *Running Without Fear* (New York: M. Evans & Co., 1985).

2. Russ Fisher, *In Search of the Funny Bone* (Houston: Rich Publishing Co., 1988).

3. Dr. Kenneth H. Cooper, *Faith-Based Fitness* (Nashville: Thomas Nelson, 1995).

CHAPTER 13

1. Dr. Ken Boa, *Reflections,* June & July 2001.

2. Albert E. N. Gray, *The Common Denominator of Success* (Falls Church, VA: National Association of Insurance & Financial Advisors), 1940.

CHAPTER 15

1. Harnett T. Kan with Inez Henry, *Miracle in the Mountains* (New York: Doubleday, 1956).

CHAPTER 16

1. Tom Hopkins, *How to Master the Art of Selling* (Scottsdale, AZ: Champion Press, 1982).

CHAPTER 17

1. *Prevention,* 1994 national survey, *Yearning to Be Stress Free . . . What Aggravates Americans Most.*

CHAPTER 18

1. Captain Scott O'Grady, *Return with Honor* (New York: Doubleday, 1995).

CHAPTER 19

1. Joe Black, *Looking Back on the Future* (Campobello, SC: Life Vision Books, 1993).

EPILOGUE

1. *USA Today,* 1 August 2001.

ABOUT THE AUTHOR

Known as *The A-Line-Mint-Specialist*, Dick Biggs works with organizations to boost bottom-line profits and better the top line—people and their productivity. He does this as a popular keynote speaker, seminar leader, facilitator, and author.

Serving smaller companies, Fortune 500s, trade associations, government agencies, public utilities, non-profit organizations, and professions such as insurance, banking and dentistry, Dick has produced results for clients in forty states, Canada, England, Germany, and Guam. His professional development topics include leadership/mentoring, communication/teamwork, empowerment, and sales. His personal growth topics include work/life balance, time/stress management, mastering change, and peak performance.

Dick is the author of *If Life Is A Balancing Act, Why Am I So Darn Clumsy?*, and the creator of *Maximize Your Moments With The Masters*, a licensed, year-long mentoring program.

Prior to launching his business in 1982, Dick was a sports writer for *The Atlanta Constitution* and the Associated Press, as well as a salesman and sales manager for thirteen years. He's a former Marine sergeant and veteran marathon runner.

A member of the National Speakers Association and past president of its Georgia chapter, Dick is married to Judy and they reside on Lake Lanier north of Atlanta. He's active in his church and is a mentor to an elementary school child in his community.

To learn more about Dick's programs and resources, please contact him at

Biggs Optimal Living Dynamics (BOLD!)
9615 Settlers Lane
Gainesville, GA 30506
770-886-3035
FAX 770-886-3017
E-mail: biggspeaks@mindspring.com
Web site: biggspeaks.com

ACKNOWLEDGMENTS

As Dr. Ken Blanchard likes to say: "None of us is as smart as all of us." This is particularly true of a book, since a great team is necessary to take an intangible concept to the tangible volume you hold in your hands.

Thank you, Robin Bennett, for introducing me to Craig Featherstone, your brother at Thomas Nelson, Inc. Craig works in the Bible Division, but he referred me to Victor Oliver. Victor is an acquisitions editor for Thomas Nelson. He believed in my idea, offered encouragement, and provided keen editorial insights.

I also appreciate Kristen Lucas, my editor at Thomas Nelson. After reading the manuscript, she said: "I like it. This is going to be a terrific project to work on." Her prediction proved true beyond my wildest imagination. She was a pleasure to work with, and I'm grateful for her valuable feedback.

My congratulations to the fine folks at The INJOY Group in Atlanta—John Maxwell, Linda Eggers, Kevin Small, and David Hoyt. Thomas Nelson has published many of John's books, so I was delighted when my friend and mentor agreed to write the foreword. Thanks, Linda, Kevin, and David, for your many useful tips.

I owe a deep gratitude to Judy, my wife. She gave me the space to work on this project when I was on a tight deadline. As chapter after chapter was produced painstakingly, Judy would say: "I'm so proud of you. I love you very much."

Finally, I'm thrilled that you've chosen to read *Burn Brightly Without Burning Out*. Please let me know how it changes your life.

Take the Steps to
BURN BRIGHTLY
WITHOUT BURNING OUT!

Biggs Optimal Living Dynamics (**BOLD!**) provides resources that
change lives and invigorate organizations:

STEP 1 Have everyone in your organization read *Burn Brightly Without Burning Out.*

This book is a powerful resource for learning the 20 life lessons on a
daily basis. And it's priced economically enough for you to purchase
copies for your entire organization.

STEP 2 Listen to *How To Balance Your Life.*

This six-cassette audio album
provides five hours of practical
application ideas for balancing
the work you need with the
life you lead.

You'll learn how to achieve
better work/life balance by
applying a simple "be-think-do-have" system that
bears this endorsement of Nightingale-Conant's Brian Tracy:
"Full of practical, easy-to-use ideas and insights that can help you be
happier and more effective — starting immediately!"

STEP 3 Arrange for a customized keynote speech or seminar.

Make your next meeting memorable by engaging Dick Biggs and **BOLD!** to deliver an inspiring keynote address or high-content seminar that produces your desired results.

In addition to popular personal growth presentations on work/life balance and stress management, **BOLD!** offers programs on time management, leadership, communication, teamwork, and mastering change.

> *"Your enthusiastic, well-prepared delivery, along with excellent study guide materials, has added structure and enduring value to the whole concept of mentoring. We are thrilled with the results."*
>
> — Julie Onstott/
>   Dick Dillon
>   Managers
>   Lucent Technologies

STEP 4 Take your professional development to the next level.

If your organization is really serious about its successor leadership, license the **BOLD!** comprehensive mentor program. *Maximize Your Moments With The Masters* is a year-long curriculum that features the following benefits for all proteges and mentors:

- Orientation session.
- 12 monthly seminars.
- Quarterly evaluations.
- Year-end celebration.
- Graduation certificate.
- Customized baton, the program symbol.
- Ongoing email access to Dick Biggs.
- Customized workbook.
- Companion reading booklet.
- Audio album.
- Train-the-trainer rights for your organization.

To place your order or to schedule an event, visit:
Biggspeaks.com